EAT DESSERT FIRST

Elise's Home Kitchen
EAT DESSERT FIRST

ELISE THOMAS founder of Cookie Co.

SHADOW
MOUNTAIN
PUBLISHING

To my mom, who taught me and gave me my passion for cooking. To my dad, who always supported me in my dreams. To my husband, Matt, who has walked every step of this journey with me and is my biggest cheerleader. To my children, who inspire me to share my passion of food with others. To my friends and family members, who never stop believing in me. And to God, who continues to write my story better than I could ever write my own.

Food photography by Yonel Cohen.

Visit us at shadowmountain.com

Library of Congress Cataloging-in-Publication Data
Names: Thomas, Elise, 1986– author.
Title: Eat dessert first / Elise Thomas.
Other titles: At head of title: Elise's home kitchen
Description: Salt Lake City : Shadow Mountain, [2024] | Includes index. | Summary: "The founder of a successful chain of bakeries shares more than 150 no-fuss recipes for delicious go-to family dinners and desserts."—Provided by publisher.
Identifiers: LCCN 2023043179 (print) | LCCN 2023043180 (ebook) | ISBN 9781639932436 (trade paperback) | ISBN 9781649332707 (ebook)
Subjects: LCSH: Cooking, American. | Desserts. | BISAC: COOKING / Courses & Dishes / General | COOKING / Courses & Dishes / Cookies | LCGFT: Cookbooks.
Classification: LCC TX715.T418 2024 (print) | LCC TX715 (ebook) | DDC 641.86—dc23/eng/20231019
LC record available at https://lccn.loc.gov/2023043179
LC ebook record available at https://lccn.loc.gov/2023043180

Printed in China
RR Donnelley, Dongguan, China

10 9 8 7 6 5 4 3 2 1

CONTENTS

COOKIES, BARS, AND TREATS

COOKIES

BARS

TREATS

the chocolate chip cookies

I can't believe I'm giving this recipe out! These are the chocolate chip cookies that brought me around to the idea of opening my own little cookie shop. Sometimes it's wild to think that franchises all over the country came from a simple recipe I've made for friends and family for years. Now you can bring joy to your loved ones too!

4 cups all-purpose flour

2 teaspoons baking soda

¼ teaspoon salt

1½ cups salted butter, softened

1¼ cups brown sugar, packed

1¼ cups granulated sugar

2 eggs

1 tablespoon pure vanilla extract

1 (12-ounce) package semisweet chocolate chips

Preheat oven to 350 degrees F. In a medium bowl, combine the flour, baking soda, and salt. Whisk and set aside.

In the bowl of a stand mixer fitted with the paddle attachment, add the butter and both sugars and mix on medium speed until light and fluffy. Add the eggs and vanilla extract and mix well. Add the flour mixture and chocolate chips and mix until flour is incorporated.

Portion the cookie dough into 2-inch balls. Set on a half-sheet baking pan, spacing them about 2 inches apart. Bake for 10–12 minutes or until the edges are lightly browned. Transfer to a cooling rack and repeat with the remaining dough.

KID FAVORITE

MAKES
2 dozen cookies

TIME
20–24 minutes

MAKES
2 dozen cookies

TIME
65 minutes

homemade oreos

I cannot be the Cookie Lady without having the best cookie recipes around. My homemade Oreos are the best you will find! They are chocolately soft cookies sandwiching a sweet cream filling. Give a plate of these to a neighbor and they are bound to feel loved.

COOKIES

2½ cups all-purpose flour

½ cup cocoa powder

1 teaspoon salt

1 teaspoon baking soda

1 cup salted butter, softened

1 cup brown sugar, packed

¾ cup granulated sugar

2 eggs

1 teaspoon pure vanilla extract

12 chocolate sandwich cookies, such as Oreos, twisted apart

FILLING

4 ounces cream cheese, softened

2 tablespoons salted butter, softened

1⅓ cups powdered sugar

1 tablespoon milk

½ teaspoon pure vanilla extract

½ teaspoon salt

Preheat oven to 350 degrees F. In a medium bowl add the flour, cocoa powder, salt, and baking soda. Whisk to combine and set aside.

In the bowl of a stand mixer fitted with the paddle attachment, add the butter and both sugars. Mix on medium speed until smooth and creamy, about 2 minutes. Add the eggs and vanilla extract. Mix well. Add the flour mixture and mix on low speed until incorporated.

Scoop the dough into 2-inch mounds. Press an Oreo cookie half into the top. Bake on a half-sheet baking pan for 8–10 minutes, being sure to not overcook. Cool cookies completely before adding filling.

To prepare the filling, add the cream cheese and butter to the bowl of a stand mixer fitted with the whisk attachment. Mix on medium speed until combined and creamy. Add the powdered sugar, milk, vanilla extract, and salt. Mix on low speed until powdered sugar is combined and then mix on high until smooth.

Spread filling onto the flat side of a cooled cookie and sandwich with the flat side of another. Store homemade Oreos in a sealed container in the refrigerator.

dino sugar cookies

My son has always loved dinosaurs. Dinosaur cookies are an easy favorite for him. He loves stomping them over the sugar cookie dough, making tracks like real dinos. This can also work great for toy car tire tracks or doll footprints too!

DOUGH

1½ cups butter, softened

2 cups granulated sugar

4 eggs

1 teaspoon pure vanilla extract

5 cups all-purpose flour

2 teaspoons baking powder

1 teaspoon cinnamon

1 teaspoon salt

TOPPING

1 tablespoon granulated sugar

1 tablespoon turbinado sugar

1 teaspoon cinnamon

Your little one's favorite dinosaur toy, car toy, or doll (cleaned well)

In a mixing bowl fitted with the paddle attachment, add the butter and sugar. Mix on medium speed until smooth and creamy. Beat in the eggs and vanilla extract until well combined. Add the flour, baking powder, cinnamon, and salt. Mix until flour is incorporated. Remove bowl from the mixer, cover with plastic wrap, and refrigerate for at least 1 hour.

Preheat oven to 400 degrees F. In a small bowl, make the topping. Add both sugars and the cinnamon and mix together. Dust your work surface with flour and roll out the chilled dough to ¼-inch thickness. Using a circle cookie cutter, cut out cookies and set on a half-sheet baking pan. Using the dinosaur toy, press the feet into the dough, making footprints. Sprinkle the topping on the footprints. Bake for 6–8 minutes or just until the underside of the cookies are lightly browned.

My son Parker helps me put the finishing touches on these cookies.

oreo-stuffed peanut butter cookies

To keep the cookies in all our Cookie Co. shops exciting, I like to create cookies that start from a totally different idea. It was the 1998 movie *The Parent Trap* with Lindsey Lohan that showed me Oreos can be dipped in peanut butter, so of course they had to become a cookie!

MAKES
2 dozen cookies

TIME
60 minutes

1 (14.3-ounce) package chocolate sandwich cookies, such as Oreos, divided

3¼ teaspoons all-purpose flour

2 teaspoons baking soda

1 teaspoon salt

1 cup salted butter, softened

1 cup smooth peanut butter

1 cup brown sugar, packed

1 cup granulated sugar

2 eggs

2 teaspoons pure vanilla extract

Set aside 24 cookies in a bowl. Put the remaining cookies in the bowl of a food processor. Pulse until crumbs. Pour into a shallow dish and set aside.

Preheat oven to 350 degrees F. In a medium bowl, combine the flour, baking soda, and salt. Whisk and set aside.

In the bowl of a stand mixer fitted with the paddle attachment, add the butter and peanut butter and mix until smooth. Add both sugars and mix on medium speed until light and fluffy. Add the eggs and vanilla extract. Mix well. Add the flour mixture and mix.

Portion the cookie dough into 2-inch balls. Wrap each ball of dough around one of the reserved Oreo cookies. Then roll the stuffed cookie dough in the Oreo crumbs. Set on a half-sheet baking pan, spacing them about 2 inches apart. Bake for 10–12 minutes, or until the edges are lightly browned. Transfer to a cooling rack and repeat with the remaining dough.

pumpkin chocolate chip cookies

At the end of summer, the moment there's the slightest chill in the air, I break out the pumpkin-scented candles. And with that comes all baked pumpkin treats too! I love the combination of pumpkin spice and chocolate. These cookies are always first on my fall baking list!

3 cups all-purpose flour

2 teaspoons pumpkin pie spice blend

1½ teaspoons baking powder

1 teaspoon baking soda

½ teaspoon salt

½ cup salted butter, softened

1 cup brown sugar, packed

2 eggs

1 cup canned pumpkin puree

1½ cups semisweet chocolate chips

1 batch Go-To Cream Cheese
   Frosting (see recipe on page 34)

Preheat oven to 350 degrees F. In a medium bowl, combine the flour, pumpkin pie spice blend, baking powder, baking soda, and salt. Whisk and set aside.

In the bowl of a stand mixer fitted with the paddle attachment, add the butter and brown sugar and mix on medium speed until light and fluffy. Add the eggs and pumpkin puree and mix well. Add the flour mixture and chocolate chips and mix until flour is incorporated.

Portion the cookie dough into 2-inch balls. Set on a half-sheet baking pan, spacing them about 2 inches apart. Bake for 10–12 minutes, or until the edges are lightly browned. Transfer to a cooling rack and repeat with the remaining dough.

Once the cookies are cooled, either spread or pipe cream cheese frosting on top.

the best sugar cookies

Making and decorating sugar cookies is one of my favorite holiday traditions with my kids. Whether it is Valentine's Day, Halloween—or even just a random weekday—we love to gather around the kitchen table with colored frosting, sprinkles, and candy and make cookies that are not only cute, but delicious too!

1½ cups salted butter, softened

2 cups granulated sugar

4 eggs

1 teaspoon pure vanilla extract

5 cups all-purpose flour

2 teaspoons baking powder

1 teaspoon salt

1 batch My Favorite Buttercream
  Frosting (see recipe on page 35)

Sprinkles and candies, for decorating

In a mixing bowl fitted with the paddle attachment, add the butter and sugar. Mix on medium speed until smooth and creamy. Beat in the eggs and vanilla extract until well combined. Add the flour, baking powder, and salt. Mix until flour is incorporated. Remove bowl from the mixer, cover with plastic wrap, and refrigerate for at least 1 hour.

Preheat oven to 400 degrees F. Dust your work surface with flour and roll out the chilled dough to ¼-inch thickness. Using your favorite cookie cutter, cut out cookies and set on a half-sheet baking pan. Bake for 6–8 minutes or just until the underside of the cookies are lightly browned.

Once the cookies are cooled, decorate with frosting, sprinkles, and candies.

COOKIES, BARS, AND TREATS

pumpkin spice squares

If you need a refresh on your usual pumpkin spice treats, here's a winner for you! Pumpkin spice squares use a yellow cake mix to give it an extra-buttery flavor. Serve it with a scoop of ice cream and caramel sauce!

Nonstick baking spray

1 (15-ounce) can pumpkin puree

1 (12-ounce) can evaporated milk

1 cup granulated sugar

3 eggs

2 teaspoons pumpkin pie spice blend

1 (15.25-ounce) box yellow cake mix

¾ cup salted butter, diced

1½ cups chopped walnuts

Preheat oven to 350 degrees F. Spray a 9x13 pan with baking spray and set aside.

In the bowl of a stand mixer fitted with the paddle attachment, add the pumpkin puree, evaporated milk, sugar, eggs, and pumpkin spice. Mix until well combined. Pour into the prepared pan, spreading it to the edges. Sprinkle the cake mix evenly on top. Finish by sprinkling the butter and walnuts over the cake mix.

Bake for 55–60 minutes or until an inserted toothpick comes out clean.

magic cookie bars

Think of all the baking staples in your pantry. Now think of putting them all together. That's pretty much what these delicious bars are. They're always a hit at any holiday cookie exchange.

1½ cups graham cracker crumbs

½ cup salted butter, melted

1 (14-ounce) can sweetened
   condensed milk

1 cup semisweet chocolate chips

1 cup butterscotch chips

1 cup shredded coconut

1 cup chopped pecans

   Preheat oven to 350 degrees F. In a medium bowl, combine the graham cracker crumbs and melted butter. Mix until combined. Press evenly into the bottom of a 9x13 baking dish. Drizzle the sweetened condensed milk over the top and spread evenly. Sprinkle the chocolate chips, butterscotch chips, coconut, and pecans on top.
   Bake for 25–30 minutes or until the coconut is browned. Allow to cool before slicing into squares.

better than boxed brownies

I'm going to go ahead and say it. These brownies are better than the ones that come from a box mix. If you don't believe me, make these and then let's talk. They are all the best things found in a perfect brownie: gooey, rich, and covered in a fluffy chocolate frosting.

KID FAVORITE

SERVES
8

TIME
60 minutes

BROWNIES

Nonstick baking spray

1 cup all-purpose flour

⅔ cup cocoa powder

½ teaspoon baking powder

½ teaspoon salt

1 cup salted butter, melted and cooled

2 cups granulated sugar

2 teaspoons pure vanilla extract

4 eggs

1 cup semisweet chocolate chips

FROSTING

2⅔ cups powdered sugar

6 tablespoons salted butter, softened

3 tablespoons cocoa powder

3 tablespoons milk

½ teaspoon pure vanilla extract

Preheat oven to 350 degrees F. Spray a 9x13 baking pan with baking spray and set aside. In a medium bowl, add the flour, cocoa powder, baking powder, and salt. Whisk and set aside.

In the bowl of a stand mixer fitted with the paddle attachment, add the melted butter, sugar, and vanilla extract. Mix on medium speed until combined. Add the eggs and mix. Add the flour mixture and chocolate chips and mix on low until well combined.

Pour the batter into the prepared pan. Bake for 30 minutes until the brownies are set on top, but still fudgy in the middle. Allow brownies to cool completely.

To prepare the frosting, add the powdered sugar, butter, and cocoa powder to a mixing bowl fitted with the whisk attachment. Mix until combined. Add the milk and vanilla extract and mix until smooth. Spread the frosting on cooled brownies.

your mom's scotcharoos

Scotcharoos are so nostalgic for me. My mom's recipe has always been the best I have had. Crisp, sweet, and topped with chocolate. They are especially yummy when they're refrigerated and cold!

Nonstick baking spray

1 cup granulated sugar

1 cup honey

1 cup creamy peanut butter

6½ cups puffed rice cereal

1½ cups semisweet chocolate chips

1 (11-ounce) bag butterscotch chips

Spray a 9x13 baking dish with baking spray. Set aside.

In a large pot over medium-high heat, add the sugar, honey, and peanut butter. Stir frequently until melted and smooth. Once the mixture begins to bubble, remove from heat and add the rice cereal. Mix well, then transfer to the prepared pan. Using wet hands, press the mixture evenly into the pan.

In a large microwave-safe bowl, add the chocolate chips and butterscotch chips. Microwave in 30-second intervals, stirring in between, until smooth. Pour on top of the rice cereal mixture and smooth with a spatula.

Refrigerate or leave at room temperature until set.

COOKIES, BARS, AND TREATS

fruit pizza

Fruit pizza is just too pretty a dessert not to love. My kids love to help decorate it with fresh fruit—and it's also a great way to get my pickier kiddos to try new fruits. This is a must for any sugar cookie lover!

CRUST

Nonstick baking spray

5½ cups all-purpose flour

1 teaspoon salt

½ teaspoon baking soda

½ teaspoon cream of tartar

1¼ cups granulated sugar

1 cup salted butter, softened

¾ cup powdered sugar

¾ cup vegetable oil

2 tablespoons water

2 eggs

2 teaspoons pure vanilla extract

1 teaspoon lemon extract

TOPPINGS

1 batch Go-To Cream Cheese Frosting (see recipe on page 34)

Blackberries

Blueberries

Kiwis, peeled and sliced

Strawberries, sliced

   Preheat oven to 350 degrees F. Spray a half-sheet baking pan with baking spray and set aside.

   In a medium bowl, add the flour, salt, baking soda, and cream of tartar. Whisk to combine. In the bowl of a stand mixer fitted with the paddle attachment, add the sugar and butter. Mix on medium speed until smooth and creamy, about 2 minutes. Add the powdered sugar, vegetable oil, water, eggs, and both extracts. Mix on medium speed until well combined. Add flour mixture and mix until the flour is incorporated.

   Using your hands, spread the dough evenly on the prepared half-sheet baking pan. Bake for 15–20 minutes until lightly browned. Allow to cool completely.

   Once cooled, spread cream cheese frosting on top and decorate with fresh fruit.

KID
FAVORITE

SERVES
8

TIME
20 minutes

hawaiian chex mix

My family is partial to sweet snack mixes instead of savory. So this Hawaiian Chex mix is right on point. It's chewy, crunchy, salty *and* sweet. I love giving out tins of this to our neighbors at Christmas.

Nonstick baking spray

1 (18-ounce) box rice squares cereal, such as Rice Chex

1 cup sweetened shredded coconut

1 cup chopped macadamia nuts

1 cup granulated sugar

1 cup light corn syrup

¾ cup salted butter

1 teaspoon almond extract

Spray a half-sheet baking pan with baking spray and set aside. In a large bowl, add the cereal, shredded coconut, and macadamia nuts.

In a medium pot over medium heat, add the sugar, corn syrup, and butter. Bring to a rolling boil and cook, stirring constantly, for 1 minute. Remove the pan from the heat and add the almond extract.

Pour the sugar mixture over the cereal mixture and stir to combine. Transfer the mix to the prepared half-sheet baking pan. Allow to cool completely before snacking.

COOKIES, BARS, AND TREATS

carolyn's caramel corn

A movie night, game night, or a championship party is not complete without my mom's caramel corn. It has the best secret ingredient: peanut butter! Just a touch of it, not much. But that's what makes it special.

½ cup popcorn kernels, popped on the stove or air-popped

2 cups brown sugar, packed

1 cup salted butter

½ cup light corn syrup

½ cup creamy peanut butter

½ teaspoon cream of tartar

1 teaspoon baking soda

Preheat oven to 250 degrees F. In a very large mixing bowl, add the popped popcorn and set aside.

In a medium pot over medium heat, add the brown sugar, butter, corn syrup, peanut butter, and cream of tartar. Cook, stirring constantly, until boiling. Remove the pot from the heat and add the baking soda. Stir until the mixture begins to puff up. Pour over the popcorn and mix well, making sure the popcorn is evenly coated in the brown sugar mixture.

Pour all the caramel popcorn on a half-sheet baking pan and bake for 30–40 minutes. If you don't eat it all in one sitting, you can store it in an airtight container or bag.

oreo truffles

Here's another Christmas treat that I like giving out to my neighbors. Oreo truffles are the perfect bite! My littles love helping dip them in chocolate—but mostly because they get to make a mess!

MAKES
24 truffles

TIME
30 minutes,
plus 2 hours
refrigeration time

1 (14.3-ounce) package chocolate sandwich cookies, such as Oreos

1 (8-ounce) package cream cheese, softened

2 cups semisweet chocolate chips

2 tablespoons vegetable shortening

1 cup white chocolate chips

Line a half-sheet baking pan with waxed or parchment paper and set aside.

In the bowl of a food processor, add the cookies. Process until the cookies are crumbs. Add the cream cheese and process until smooth and well combined.

Roll the cookie mixture into 2-inch balls and set on the prepared half-sheet baking pan. Refrigerate until firm, about 2 hours.

In a medium bowl, add the chocolate chips and the shortening. Microwave for 30 seconds at a time, stirring in between, until smooth. Using two forks, dip each truffle in the melted chocolate and set back on the half-sheet baking pan.

Once all the truffles have been dipped in chocolate, add the white chocolate chips to a small bowl. Microwave in the same manner as the semisweet chocolate chips. Using a fork or a wire whisk, drizzle white chocolate over each truffle. Refrigerate until set.

MAKES
2 cups

TIME
15 minutes

your mom's hot fudge sauce

A plain scoop of vanilla ice cream feels so much more special with hot fudge sauce. This one comes together in a snap with basic pantry ingredients. We love banana splits at my house, so this sauce is a must!

½ cup salted butter

1 cup evaporated milk

1 cup semisweet chocolate chips

1 cup powdered sugar

1 teaspoon pure vanilla extract

In a small saucepan over medium heat, add the butter and evaporated milk, stirring occasionally. Once the butter is melted, add the chocolate chips. Stir constantly until the chocolate chips are melted. Add powdered sugar. Stir constantly until boiling.

Remove from heat and stir in the vanilla extract.

CAKES AND PIES

CAKES

PIES

MAKES
enough frosting for
24 cupcakes or a
two-layer 9-inch cake

TIME
20 minutes

go-to cream cheese frosting

Just like everyone needs a reliable buttercream frosting recipe, a cream cheese frosting recipe is essential too. What is carrot cake, cinnamon rolls, or fruit pizza without it? My go-to cream cheese frosting recipe will soon be yours as well!

1 (8-ounce) package cream cheese, softened

¼ cup salted butter, softened

2¾ cups powdered sugar

2 tablespoons milk

1 teaspoon pure vanilla extract

1 teaspoon salt

   In the bowl of a stand mixer fitted with the whisk attachment, add the cream cheese and butter. Mix on medium speed until combined and creamy. Add the powdered sugar, milk, vanilla extract, and salt. Mix on low speed until powdered sugar is combined and then mix on high until smooth.

my favorite buttercream frosting

MAKES
enough frosting for
24 cupcakes or a
two-layer 9-inch cake

Whether it's a birthday cake, celebration cupcakes, or perfect sugar cookies, you always need a perfect buttercream frosting recipe. Many years of experience in making sweet treats has led me to create my favorite one. You can sub in any kind of flavoring extract you like to make it your own. Whatever you choose to do with this buttercream frosting, you can bet it will become your favorite recipe too!

TIME
20 minutes

½ cup salted butter, softened

2¾ cups powdered sugar

3 tablespoons milk

1 teaspoon pure vanilla extract

½ teaspoon salt

Add the butter to the bowl of a stand mixer fitted with the whisk attachment. Mix on medium speed until smooth. Add the powdered sugar, milk, vanilla extract, and salt. Mix on low speed until the powdered sugar is combined and then mix on high until smooth.

abbi's funfetti birthday cake

I have only one daughter, so I look forward to making a really girly cake when her birthday rolls around. Even when she's an adult and long past her childhood, you can bet I'll still make her a funfetti cake.

Nonstick baking spray

3 cups cake flour

1 tablespoon baking powder

1 teaspoon salt

1 cup salted butter, melted and cooled

1¾ cups granulated sugar

6 egg whites

1 tablespoon clear vanilla extract

1 teaspoon butter extract

1 cup buttermilk

½ cup sour cream

½ cup rainbow sprinkles, plus more for decoration

1 batch My Favorite Buttercream Frosting (see recipe on page 35)

Preheat oven to 350 degrees F. Spray three 9-inch cake pans with baking spray and set aside.

In a medium bowl, combine the flour, baking powder, and salt. Whisk well to combine and set aside. In the bowl of a stand mixer fitted with the whisk attachment, add the butter, sugar, egg whites, and both extracts. Mix on medium speed until smooth and well combined, about 2 minutes. Add the flour mixture and mix well. Add the buttermilk, sour cream, and sprinkles. Mix on medium speed until smooth and creamy.

Pour the cake batter into the three prepared pans, being sure to split it as evenly as you can. Bake for 30–45 minutes, or until an inserted toothpick comes out clean. Set the cakes aside to cool completely.

Using the buttercream frosting, stack the cakes and sandwich with frosting. Decorate with more rainbow sprinkles.

My daughter, Abbi, loves to help me make cakes.

pretty in pink vanilla cake

Making birthday cakes for my friends is my way of making them feel extra special on their big day. Birthdays as an adult just don't have the same excitement, you know what I mean? But a tall, pink-frosted cake can bring back all that childhood birthday magic!

Nonstick baking spray

2¾ cups cake flour

1 tablespoon baking powder

¾ teaspoon salt

1 cup salted butter, softened

1¾ cups granulated sugar

3 eggs, at room temperature

1 cup milk, at room temperature

½ cup sour cream, at room temperature

2 teaspoons pure vanilla extract

Red food coloring

1 batch My Favorite Buttercream Frosting (see recipe on page 35)

Preheat oven to 350 degrees F. Spray three 6-inch cake pans with baking spray and set aside.

In a medium bowl, add the flour, baking powder, and salt. Whisk to combine and set aside. In the bowl of a stand mixer fitted with the paddle attachment, add the butter and sugar. Mix on medium speed until smooth and well combined, about 2 minutes. Add the eggs, milk, sour cream, and vanilla extract. Mix on low until well combined.

Add a few drops of red food coloring to make a light pink and mix in by hand. Pour a third of the batter into one of the prepared pans. Add a few more drops of red food coloring to make a brighter pink and pour half of that batter into another of the prepared pans. Finally, add more red food coloring to make a darker pink. Add that to the last prepared pan.

Bake all three pans for 35–40 minutes, or until an inserted toothpick comes out clean. Cool completely before assembling and frosting with buttercream.

sour cream crumb cake

This sour cream crumb cake is the best brunch dish. Not quite coffee cake, not quite dessert. Perfect to make ahead, perfect to share with a neighbor. If you're feeling fancy, some fresh blueberries mixed into the batter would be bliss.

CRUMB TOPPING

2¼ cups all-purpose flour

1 cup granulated sugar

½ cup brown sugar, packed

½ teaspoon salt

1½ teaspoons cinnamon

1 cup salted butter, melted

1 teaspoon pure vanilla extract

CAKE

Nonstick baking spray

2 cups all-purpose flour

1 teaspoon baking powder

½ teaspoon baking soda

½ teaspoon salt

½ cup salted butter, softened

1 cup granulated sugar

1 cup sour cream

2 eggs

1 teaspoon pure vanilla extract

2 cups cold heavy cream,
  for whipped topping

¼ cup powdered sugar, for
  whipped topping

In a medium bowl, add all of the crumb topping ingredients, mix by hand and set aside.

Preheat oven to 350 degrees F. Spray a 9x13 pan with baking spray. In a medium bowl, combine the flour, baking powder, baking soda, and salt. Whisk together and set aside.

To prepare the cake, add the butter and sugar to the bowl of a stand mixer fitted with the paddle attachment. Mix on medium speed until smooth and creamy. Mix in the sour cream, eggs, and vanilla extract. Add the flour mixture and mix until the flour is well combined. Pour the batter into the prepared pan and smooth the top. Sprinkle the crumb topping on top of the batter. Bake for 30–35 minutes, or until an inserted toothpick comes out clean.

Before serving, add the heavy cream and the powdered sugar to the bowl of a stand mixer fitted with the whisk attachment. Mix on medium speed until soft peaks form. Serve cake with a dollop of whipped cream.

the ultimate chocolate bundt cake

This gooey, chocolatey, caramel-y cake is a New Year's Eve tradition. By the time the clock strikes midnight, I have had more slices than I will admit to! And rumor has it that this cake tastes even better for breakfast the next day.

CAKE

Nonstick baking spray

1 (15.25-ounce) box chocolate cake mix

1 (3.9-ounce) box instant chocolate pudding, such as Jell-O

1 cup vegetable oil

1 cup water

3 eggs

1 cup semisweet chocolate chips

GLAZE

1 cup powdered sugar

¼ cup cocoa powder

2 tablespoons salted butter, melted

½ teaspoon pure vanilla extract

Hot water

1 (11-ounce) jar caramel sauce topping

½ cup white chocolate chips

Gold sprinkles

Preheat oven to 350 degrees F. Spray a Bundt pan with baking spray and set aside.

In a blender, add the cake mix, instant pudding, vegetable oil, water, and eggs. Mix on medium speed until smooth and well combined. Pour into prepared pan. Sprinkle chocolate chips over the batter and stir lightly with a spoon to incorporate them.

Bake for 45–50 minutes or until an inserted toothpick comes out clean. Allow the cake to cool in the pan for 20 minutes and then invert onto a cooling rack. Set the cooling rack on a half-sheet baking pan.

To prepare the glaze, add the powdered sugar, cocoa powder, melted butter, and vanilla extract in a medium bowl. Using a hand mixer, mix until smooth. Add a teaspoon of hot water until the glaze is the desired consistency. Drizzle over the cooled cake.

Warm up the jar of caramel sauce in the microwave in 30-second intervals until it's pourable. Drizzle over the chocolate glaze.

Add white chocolate chips to a small bowl. Microwave at 30-second intervals until smooth. Drizzle over the chocolate and caramel glaze. Decorate with gold sprinkles. Allow toppings to set before serving.

texas sheet cake

It's 45 minutes before you're supposed to leave for a family gathering and you forgot you've been asked to bring dessert. No worries! Texas sheet cake is your best friend. Not only does it come together and bake quickly, but you can put the frosting on it while it's still warm (and let it cool in the car). Unfortunately, you will likely not have leftovers, so I recommend cutting out a piece to save at home before you leave!

SERVES
12

TIME
45 minutes

CAKE

Nonstick baking spray

2 cups all-purpose flour

2 cups granulated sugar

1 cup water

½ cup salted butter

½ cup vegetable shortening

⅓ cup cocoa powder

½ cup buttermilk

2 eggs

1 teaspoon baking soda

1 teaspoon pure vanilla extract

FROSTING

½ cup salted butter

¼ cup cocoa powder

2 tablespoons milk

2½ cups powdered sugar

1 cup mini chocolate candies, such as M&M's

Preheat oven to 400 degrees F. Spray a half-sheet baking pan with baking spray and set aside.

To prepare the cake, add the flour and sugar to a large bowl. Whisk together and set aside. In a medium saucepan over medium heat, add the water, butter, shortening, and cocoa powder. Once the butter is melted, whisk well and then pour it over the flour mixture and stir. Add the buttermilk, eggs, baking soda, and vanilla extract. Mix well by hand or with a hand mixer.

Pour the cake batter into the prepared pan, spreading it evenly to the corners. Bake for 20 minutes.

While the cake bakes, prepare the frosting. In the same saucepan used for the butter/shortening/cocoa powder mixture, add the butter, cocoa powder, and milk. Bring to a simmer over medium heat. Once the butter has melted, remove the pan from the heat and add the powdered sugar. Mix with a hand mixer on medium speed until smooth.

Once the cake is out of the oven, pour the frosting over the warm cake. Sprinkle M&M's on top. Allow to cool completely before serving.

cookies & cream icebox cake

SERVES
12

TIME
45 minutes

This is one of my favorite make-ahead summer treats. It's sure useful to have one in the freezer ready to go for a special treat when my family needs a pick-me-up. This is also a very flexible recipe—you can switch up the ice cream flavor or the type of cookies used. Mint chip ice cream would be amazing!

1 cup salted butter, divided

1 (14.3-ounce) package chocolate sandwich cookies, such as Oreos, crushed in the food processor or blender

1 (128-ounce) bucket vanilla ice cream, softened

1 batch Your Mom's Hot Fudge Sauce (see recipe on page 30), cooled

1 (8-ounce) tub whipped topping, such as Cool Whip

1 (1.55-ounce) chocolate bar, such as Hershey's, shaved with a vegetable peeler

Preheat oven to 350 degrees F.

In a medium saucepan over medium-high heat, melt ½ cup butter. Once the butter is melted, remove the pan from the heat and add the crushed Oreos. Stir until combined. Press the mixture into the bottom of a 9x13 baking pan. Bake for 15 minutes. Cool completely.

Once the crust has cooled, evenly spread the vanilla ice cream on top. Put the pan in the freezer.

Once the vanilla ice cream has set, spread the fudge sauce evenly over the vanilla ice cream layer and return the pan to the freezer.

Once the chocolate sauce is frozen, spread the whipped topping and then sprinkle chocolate shavings on top.

CAKES AND PIES

47

caramel cookie icebox cake

My mother ate this delicious ice cream dessert at a church function and wouldn't leave until she'd found who made it and got the recipe. She's adapted it a bit, and it became a Sunday dessert family favorite in our home. My mom's sisters call her to this day to get the recipe when they can't find it. It's a yummy cookie caramel ice cream dessert that's sure to impress all guests.

Nonstick baking spray

1 cup salted butter, melted

2 cups all-purpose flour

1 cup chopped walnuts

½ cup brown sugar, packed

½ cup quick oats

½ teaspoon salt

1 (11-ounce) jar caramel sauce
   topping, divided

1 (128-ounce) bucket vanilla
   ice cream, softened

Preheat oven to 350 degrees F. Spray a half-sheet baking pan with baking spray and set aside.

In the bowl of a stand mixer fitted with the paddle attachment, add the butter, flour, walnuts, brown sugar, oats, and salt. Mix on medium speed until well combined. Evenly press the cookie dough mixture into the prepared pan. Bake for 20 minutes, or until the edges are lightly browned. Set aside to cool completely.

Once cooled, crumble the cookie into tiny pieces. Sprinkle half of it in a 9x13 baking pan. Drizzle half the caramel sauce over the top. Spread softened ice cream over the caramel, spreading evenly to the edges of the pan. Add the remaining cookie crumbles over the ice cream and drizzle the remaining caramel sauce, then freeze until solid.

chocolate satin pie

Pumpkin pie has its place on a Thanksgiving table, but given the choice, I'm going for the chocolate satin pie. I love this cold, creamy dessert after a heavy helping of turkey, mashed potatoes, gravy, and all the things that come with it. I have a feeling you'll feel the same!

¾ cup salted butter, softened and divided

1 (14.3-ounce) package chocolate sandwich cookies, such as Oreos, crushed in the food processor or blender

12 ounces cream cheese, softened

½ cup granulated sugar

1½ cups semisweet chocolate chips

1 (8-ounce) tub whipped topping, such as Cool Whip, divided

1 (1.55-ounce) chocolate bar, such as Hershey's, shaved with a vegetable peeler

Preheat oven to 350 degrees F. In a large bowl, add ½ cup of the butter. Microwave in 10-second increments until melted. Add crushed cookies and mix well. Pour mixture into a 9-inch pie pan and press evenly along the bottom and the sides. Bake for 8–10 minutes until set. Set aside to cool.

In the bowl of a stand mixer fitted with the paddle attachment, add the remaining ¼ cup softened butter, the cream cheese, and the sugar. Mix on medium speed until smooth and creamy. In a small microwave-safe bowl, add the chocolate chips. Microwave in 30-second intervals, stirring in between until smooth. Add to the cream cheese mixture and mix until well combined. With a rubber scraper, fold in 2 cups whipped topping. Pour into prepared cookie crust and smooth the top. Add the remaining whipped topping and top with chocolate shavings.

Refrigerate for at least 4 hours, or until set.

CAKES AND PIES

lemon blackberry pie

Pie Night is one of my favorite traditions with my friends. We invite friends over, and everyone brings a pie. Ideally they also bring the recipe! My friend once brought a lemon blueberry pie and I knew I needed to add that to my dessert recipe collection!

CRUST

1½ cups graham cracker crumbs

⅓ cup granulated sugar

6 tablespoons salted butter, melted

BLACKBERRY SAUCE

3 cups fresh or frozen blackberries

¾ cup granulated sugar

¾ cup water

3 tablespoons cornstarch

1 teaspoon lemon juice

LEMON TOPPING

1 (8-ounce) package cream cheese, softened

⅓ cup granulated sugar

1 tablespoon lemon zest

2 teaspoons lemon juice

1 cup heavy cream

Preheat oven to 350 degrees F. In a medium bowl, combine all the crust ingredients and mix until well combined. Pour the crust mixture into a 9-inch pie pan and press along the bottom and sides. Bake for 8–10 minutes until lightly browned. Once baked, set aside to cool slightly.

For the blackberry sauce, add the blackberries, sugar, water, cornstarch, and lemon juice to a medium saucepan over medium heat. Bring mixture to a simmer, stirring constantly while also mashing the berries. Cook until thickened, about 5 minutes. Allow to cool completely in the refrigerator.

For the lemon topping, using a hand mixer, stir together the cream cheese, sugar, lemon zest, and lemon juice. Add the heavy cream to the bowl of a stand mixer fitted with the whisk attachment. Mix on medium speed until stiff peaks form. Fold in the cream cheese mixer with a spatula until smooth and well combined.

To assemble the pie, add the cooled blackberry sauce to the prepared crust. Smooth the top and then add the lemon topping. Refrigerate for at least 2 hours before serving.

take me back key lime pie

Any time a dessert is named after a vacation destination, I am on board. I went on a vacation to Key West in the Florida Keys with my husband a few years ago, and I can confirm that their signature pie is worthy of all the praise. I came home determined to recreate that creamy, tart delight. It is a must-try!

CRUST

1½ cups graham cracker crumbs

⅓ cup granulated sugar

6 tablespoons salted butter, melted

FILLING

2 (14-ounce) cans sweetened condensed milk

½ cup sour cream

3 egg yolks

½ cup bottled key lime juice, such as Nellie and Joe's Famous

Zest of 1 lime

TOPPING

1½ cups heavy cream

3 tablespoons granulated sugar

1 teaspoon pure vanilla extract

¼ cup sliced almonds

1 lime, sliced

Preheat oven to 350 degrees F. In a medium bowl, combine all crust ingredients. Mix until well combined. Add the crust mixture to a 9-inch pie pan and press along the bottom and sides. Bake for 8–10 minutes until lightly browned. Once baked, set aside to cool slightly.

In the bowl of a stand mixer fitted with the whisk attachment, add all the filling ingredients. Mix on medium speed until smooth and well combined. Pour into the cooled crust. Bake for 15 minutes until the filling is set. Allow to cool completely in the refrigerator.

For the topping, add the heavy cream, sugar, and vanilla extract to the bowl of a stand mixer fitted with the whisk attachment. Mix on medium speed until soft peaks form, about 5 minutes. Spread or pipe the whipped cream onto the top of the refrigerated pie. Garnish with sliced almonds and lime slices.

BREADS

SWEET BREADS

SAVORY BREADS

cinnamon nutella swirl bread

What's better than a fresh, warm slice of white bread? A fresh, warm slice of white bread filled with Nutella and cinnamon! If you happen to have any leftovers, it makes great French toast.

MAKES
2 loaves

TIME
65–70 minutes,
plus 1½–2 hours
rising time

Nonstick baking spray

2 cups warm water (between 120–130 degrees F.)

½ cup granulated sugar

1½ tablespoons instant yeast

1½ teaspoons salt

¼ cup vegetable oil

6 cups all-purpose flour, divided

2 cups chocolate hazelnut spread, such as Nutella, divided

4 teaspoons cinnamon, divided

Softened butter, for brushing after baking

Spray 2 (9x5) loaf pans with baking spray and set aside.

In the bowl of a stand mixer fitted with the dough hook attachment, add the water, sugar, and yeast. Using a whisk, mix them together until combined. Let sit for 7 minutes. The yeast should create foam on top of the water. Add the salt, vegetable oil, and half the flour. Mix on low speed until the flour is incorporated. Once the flour is incorporated into the dough, add the remaining flour in ½-cup increments and mix until the dough pulls away from the sides of the bowl. It should feel slightly sticky and soft. You may not need all of the remaining flour.

Remove the dough from the bowl and spray the bowl with baking spray. Put the dough back in, cover with plastic wrap, and let rise for 1 hour, until doubled in size. Once risen, cut the dough in half. Roll each loaf into a 9x9-inch square. Spread 1 cup of chocolate hazelnut spread on each square, then sprinkle with 2 teaspoons of cinnamon. Roll up each square and shape into a loaf, leaving a seam underneath the loaf so the top is smooth. Place each loaf into a prepared pan and let rise for an additional 30–40 minutes.

Preheat oven to 350 degrees F. Bake loaves for 20–25 minutes. Once baked, brush butter on top of each loaf.

MAKES
12 rolls

TIME
About 3½ hours,
including rising time

cinnamon rolls with cream cheese frosting

Want to be everyone's favorite? Make some cinnamon rolls. Whether it is an after-school surprise, a lazy weekend morning, or an alternative for a birthday cake, warm cinnamon rolls covered in cream cheese frosting are both indulgent and comforting.

DOUGH

1 cup milk

1 tablespoon active dry yeast

2 eggs

1 egg yolk

½ cup salted butter, melted and cooled

⅓ cup granulated sugar

1 teaspoon salt

4 cups all-purpose flour

Nonstick baking spray

FILLING

½ cup salted butter, melted

1 cup brown sugar, packed

1 tablespoon cinnamon

FROSTING

¼ cup salted butter, softened

4 ounces cream cheese, softened

1 teaspoon salt

1 teaspoon pure vanilla extract

2 tablespoons milk

4 cups powdered sugar

Microwave the milk in 30-second intervals until it reaches 100–110 degrees F. Pour into the bowl of a stand mixer fitted with the paddle attachment. Add the yeast, eggs, yolk, butter, sugar, and salt. Mix on low until combined. Change to the dough hook attachment. Mix on low while adding the flour in ½-cup increments. Once combined, knead on low for 5 minutes. Remove the dough from the bowl and spray the bowl with baking spray. Put the dough back in, cover with plastic wrap, and let rise for 2 hours until doubled in size.

Spray a 9x13 pan with baking spray and set aside. Dust your countertop with flour. Roll the dough out into a 24x12-inch rectangle. In a small bowl, combine all the filling ingredients and spread on the dough. Starting from the top, roll the dough down to the bottom, making sure it's rolled tightly, pinching the

My son Ryker loves cinnamon rolls!

dough once you get to the end. Cut the dough in half with a sharp knife, baking twine, or unflavored dental floss, then divide each half into 6 rolls.

Place each roll in the prepared pan. Cover with a towel and let rise for 30–45 minutes. Preheat oven to 375 degrees F. and bake for 15–20 minutes until tops are lightly browned. While the rolls bake, make the frosting. In a mixing bowl, combine the butter, cream cheese, salt, vanilla extract, milk, and powdered sugar. Mix on medium until smooth. Spread frosting over warm rolls.

chocolate chip pecan pumpkin bread

I recommend doubling this recipe so you have an extra loaf to share with a friend or neighbor. Who wouldn't be thrilled with a warm loaf of the best bread for fall?

Nonstick baking spray

1½ cups all-purpose flour

2 teaspoons pumpkin pie spice blend

1 teaspoon baking soda

¾ teaspoon salt

1½ cups granulated sugar

½ cup vegetable oil

2 eggs

1 teaspoon pure vanilla extract

1 cup canned pumpkin puree

1 cup semisweet chocolate chips

1 cup chopped pecans

Preheat oven to 350 degrees F. Spray a 9x5 loaf pan with baking spray and set aside.

In a medium bowl, add the flour, pumpkin pie spice blend, baking soda, and salt. Whisk well to combine and set aside.

In the bowl of a stand mixer fitted with the paddle attachment, add the sugar, vegetable oil, eggs, vanilla, and pumpkin puree. Mix on medium speed until well combined and smooth. Fold in the flour mixture, chocolate chips, and pecans until well combined.

Pour batter into the prepared pan. Bake for 55–60 minutes or until an inserted toothpick comes out clean.

MAKES
12 rolls

TIME
45 minutes,
plus 2–3 hours
rising time

orange sweet rolls

The city where I live in Southern California is famous for having been mostly orange groves decades ago. There aren't as many groves as there used to be, so locals make up for it by baking all kinds of delicious orange-flavored treats. My personal favorite are orange sweet rolls. They'll be your favorite too.

DOUGH

½ cup milk

½ cup orange juice

1 tablespoon active dry yeast

2 eggs

1 egg yolk

½ cup salted butter, melted and cooled

⅓ cup granulated sugar

1 teaspoon salt

4 cups all-purpose flour

Nonstick baking spray

FILLING

½ cup salted butter, melted

⅔ cup granulated sugar

⅓ cup brown sugar, packed

2 tablespoons orange zest

GLAZE

2 cups powdered sugar

2 tablespoons orange juice

2 tablespoons salted butter, melted

1 tablespoon orange zest

½ teaspoon pure vanilla extract

½ teaspoon orange extract

Microwave the milk in 30-second intervals until it reaches 100–110 degrees F. Pour into the bowl of a stand mixer fitted with the paddle attachment. Add the orange juice, yeast, eggs, yolk, butter, sugar, and salt. Mix on low until combined. Change to the dough hook attachment. Mix on low while adding the flour in ½-cup increments. Knead on low for 5 minutes. Remove the dough from the bowl and spray the bowl with baking spray. Put the dough back in, cover with plastic wrap, and let rise for 2 hours until doubled in size.

Spray a 9x13 pan with baking spray and set aside. Dust your countertop with flour. Roll dough out into a 24x12 rectangle. In a small bowl, combine all the filling ingredients and spread on the dough. Starting from the top, roll the dough down to the bottom, being sure it is rolled tightly, pinching the dough once you get to the end. Cut the dough in half with a sharp knife, baking twine, or unflavored dental floss, then divide each half into 6 rolls.

Place each roll in the prepared pan. Cover with a towel and let rise for 30–45 minutes. Preheat oven to 375 degrees F. Bake for 15–20 minutes, until tops are lightly browned.

While the rolls bake, make the glaze. In a medium bowl, add all the glaze ingredients and whisk until smooth. Spread glaze over warm rolls.

your mom's banana bread

Banana bread was a staple of my childhood. We weren't ever sad when bananas went brown. On the contrary—my mom would buy more than she knew we'd eat so that they could become banana bread. This recipe is the best one I have ever had!

Nonstick baking spray

2 cups all-purpose flour

1½ teaspoons baking powder

½ teaspoon baking soda

¼ teaspoon salt

1 cup granulated sugar

½ cup salted butter, melted and cooled

2 eggs

¾ cup milk

1 teaspoon lemon juice

2 overly ripe bananas, mashed

KID FAVORITE

MAKES
1 loaf

TIME
70–75 minutes

Preheat oven to 350 degrees F. Spray a 9x5 loaf pan with baking spray and set aside.

In a medium bowl, add the flour, baking powder, baking soda, and salt. Whisk well to combine and set aside.

In the bowl of a stand mixer fitted with the paddle attachment, add the sugar, melted butter, eggs, milk, and lemon juice. Mix on medium speed until well combined and smooth. Add mashed bananas. Add flour mixture until well combined.

Pour batter into the prepared pan. Bake for 55–60 minutes or until an inserted toothpick comes out clean.

basic cornbread

You can't have chili without cornbread. I think that might even be illegal in some states. All kidding aside, there is a reason it's the perfect partner to your favorite chili or chowder. I like to crumble it on top of my soup so I get a little cornbread in each bite!

Nonstick baking spray

1 cup all-purpose flour

1 cup cornmeal

⅔ cup granulated sugar

3½ teaspoons baking powder

1 teaspoon salt

1 egg

1 cup milk

⅓ cup vegetable oil

1 cup frozen corn kernels

Preheat oven to 400 degrees F. Spray a 9x13 baking pan with baking spray and set aside.

In the bowl of a stand mixer fitted with the paddle attachment, add the flour, cornmeal, sugar, baking powder, and salt. Mix on low speed until combined. Add the egg, milk, and vegetable oil. Mix on medium speed until well combined. Stir in the frozen corn.

Pour the cornbread batter into the prepared pan. Bake for 20–25 minutes or until an inserted toothpick comes out clean.

herbed artisan bread

The magic of water, flour, and yeast is something I will never stop being amazed by. The simplest of ingredients put together in just the right way yields one of the most satisfying results. With this bread, I like adding a few dried herbs to pump up the flavor. It's ideal next to a bowl of soup or even for making grilled cheese sandwiches.

1½ cups warm water (between 120–130 degrees F.)

2¼ teaspoons instant yeast

3¾ cups bread flour, divided

2 teaspoons dried rosemary

1 teaspoon dried sage

1 teaspoon dried oregano

2 teaspoons salt

Nonstick baking spray

In the bowl of a stand mixer fitted with the dough hook attachment, add the water and yeast. Using a whisk, mix them together until combined. Let sit for 7 minutes. The yeast should create foam on top of the water. Add 2 cups of the flour, the rosemary, sage, oregano, and salt. Mix on low speed until the flour is incorporated. Once the flour is incorporated into the dough, add the remaining flour in ½-cup increments until the dough pulls away from the sides of the bowl. It should feel slightly sticky and soft.

Remove the dough from the bowl and spray the bowl with baking spray. Put the dough back in, cover with plastic wrap, and let rise for 1½–2 hours until doubled in size.

Preheat the oven to 450 degrees F. While the oven preheats, put a large oven-proof Dutch oven in with the lid on. Allow the Dutch oven to preheat for at least 30 minutes.

Lay a sheet of parchment paper on the counter and sprinkle with flour. Using lightly floured hands, reach down one side of the dough to the bottom of the bowl, pull up and stretch the edge of the dough over the center toward the opposite side. Turn the bowl and repeat the folding and turning, working in a circle around the dough until it starts to hold its shape, about 8 to 10 rotations. Turn out the dough onto the parchment, placing it seam side down. Shape into a round loaf. Cover with a towel and let rest for 10 minutes.

Using a sharp knife or a bread lame, cut a few slashes into the top of the loaf. Take the Dutch oven from the oven, remove lid, then carefully place the dough with the parchment paper directly into the preheated Dutch oven. Cover with the lid.

Bake for 30 minutes, then remove the lid and bake until deeply browned, about 15 minutes more. Carefully remove the loaf from the Dutch oven and place it on a cooling rack. Let cool for 20 minutes before slicing.

pretzel bites

Any recipe labeled with the world "bite" is always going to be trouble for me. My brain immediately thinks "just one more" and before I know it, I've eaten half the batch! Luckily, my family loves these pretzel bites as much as I do. I couldn't polish them all off even if I tried!

KID
FAVORITE

MAKES
about 60 pretzel bites

TIME
60 minutes

DOUGH

1½ cups warm water (between 100–110 degrees F.)

1 tablespoon brown sugar, packed

1 (.75-ounce) packet active dry yeast

1 teaspoon salt

2 tablespoons salted butter, melted and cooled

4 cups all-purpose flour

WATER BATH

2 quarts water

½ cup baking soda

In the bowl of a stand mixer fitted with the dough hook attachment, add the water, sugar, yeast, and salt. Using a whisk, mix them together until combined. Let sit for 7 minutes. The yeast should create foam on top of the water. Add the cooled butter and mix. With the mixer on low speed, gradually add the flour in ½-cup increments. Once the flour is incorporated into the dough, the dough should pull away from the sides of the bowl. It should feel slightly sticky and soft. Knead the dough for 5 minutes. Allow to rest for 10 minutes.

To prepare the water bath, add the water and baking soda to a large pot over high heat. Bring to a boil. While you wait, divide the dough in half. Then divide each half into three equal portions. Roll each portion into a long rope. Cut the dough into small 1 oz. balls.

Once the water is boiling, gently lower the dough balls into the water and boil for 15 seconds. Remove from heat and place on a half-sheet baking pan.

Preheat oven to 400 degrees F.

Bake the pretzel bits for 13–15 minutes, until browned.

MAKES
24 rolls

TIME
About 2½ hours,
including rising time

my mom's dinner rolls

If you don't yet have a favorite dinner roll recipe, you should be so stoked, because my mom has the best one! I especially love making these for Sunday dinners. And if there's gravy involved with that, even better!

2 cups warm water (between 100–110 degrees F.)

2 tablespoons active dry yeast

¼ cup granulated sugar

2 eggs

2 teaspoons salt

4½ cups all-purpose flour

Nonstick baking spray

6 tablespoons salted butter, melted

In the bowl of a stand mixer fitted with the dough hook, add the water and yeast. Using a whisk, mix them together by hand until combined. Let sit for 7 minutes. The yeast should create foam on top of the water.

In a small bowl, combine sugar, eggs, and salt and whisk until combined. Add to the yeast in the mixer bowl. Add half the flour. Mix on low speed until the flour is incorporated. Once the flour is incorporated into the dough, add the remaining flour in ½-cup increments until the dough pulls away from the sides of the bowl. It should feel slightly sticky and soft. You may not need all of the remaining flour.

This is my mom's delicious recipe!

Remove the dough from the bowl and spray the bowl with baking spray. Put the dough back in, cover with plastic wrap, and let rise for 30 minutes. Punch down and allow to rise two more times.

Pour the melted butter into a 9x13 baking pan. Divide the dough in half. Roll each half into a ½-inch thick rope. Cut each rope into 12 even pieces. You will have 24 balls of dough. Place the dough balls evenly in the 9x13 pan and let rise for 15 minutes.

Preheat oven to 375 degrees F. Bake the rolls for 20–25 minutes.

BREAKFAST AND BRUNCH

BREAKFAST

BRUNCH

chocolate chip wheat muffins

MAKES
12 muffins

TIME
40–45 minutes

Everything goes down easier with chocolate, don't you think? My family has no idea they're eating something that's good for them if chocolate is involved.

1 cup all-purpose flour

1 cup wheat germ

2 teaspoons baking powder

¼ teaspoon salt

1 cup brown sugar, packed

½ cup vegetable oil

2 eggs

1 cup sour cream

½ teaspoon pure vanilla extract

1 cup mini chocolate chips

Oats, for sprinkling on the muffins

Preheat oven to 350 degrees F. Place muffin liners into a muffin pan and set aside.

In a medium bowl, add the flour, wheat germ, baking powder, and salt. Whisk and set aside.

In the bowl of a stand mixer fitted with the paddle attachment, add the brown sugar, vegetable oil, and eggs. Mix on medium speed until combined. Add the sour cream and vanilla extract. Mix on medium speed until combined. Add the flour mixture and chocolate chips. Mix on low speed until well combined.

Portion the muffin batter into the prepared muffin liners. Sprinkle oats on top. Bake for 15–20 minutes, or until an inserted toothpick comes out clean.

coffee cake muffins

It's okay, you can admit it. You like coffee cake just for the buttery streusel on top. Me too! I will always eat the top of these muffins first! Luckily the rest is delicious too!

STREUSEL TOPPING

½ cup all-purpose flour

½ cup brown sugar, packed

¼ cup salted butter, sliced

1 teaspoon cinnamon

MUFFINS

2¼ cups all-purpose flour

2 teaspoons baking powder

½ teaspoon baking soda

¼ teaspoon salt

1 cup granulated sugar

⅓ cup salted butter, softened

1 cup sour cream

⅓ cup vegetable oil

2 eggs

2 teaspoons pure vanilla extract

Preheat oven to 350 degrees F. Place muffin liners into a muffin pan and set aside.

For the streusel topping, in a medium bowl, add the flour, brown sugar, butter, and cinnamon. Using a pastry blender, cut the butter into the flour mixture until the butter is the size of small pebbles. Set aside.

My son Reagan loves these muffins!

For the muffins, in a medium bowl, add the flour, baking powder, baking soda, and salt. Whisk together and set aside. In the bowl of a stand mixer fitted with the paddle attachment, add the sugar and butter. Mix on medium speed until smooth and creamy. Add the sour cream, vegetable oil, eggs, and vanilla extract. Mix on medium speed until well combined.

Portion the muffin batter into the prepared muffin liners. Sprinkle the streusel topping on top of each muffin. Bake for 18–20 minutes, or until an inserted toothpick comes out clean.

baked french toast

Christmas morning breakfast (or brunch) is made easy with this baked French toast. I can get this prepped and put in the fridge while my husband and I wait for our excited kids to fall asleep so Santa Claus can come. Of course my kids wake us up way too early and I am always glad I took a few minutes the night before to have this ready to pop in the oven in the morning.

KID FAVORITE

MAKES
8 servings

TIME
12 hours (break this up with cook and refrigerator time)

FRENCH TOAST

2 tablespoons salted butter, softened

1 (15-ounce) loaf sourdough bread, sliced

8 eggs

2 cups milk

½ cup brown sugar, packed

½ cup granulated sugar

½ cup heavy cream

2 tablespoons pure vanilla extract

CRUMBLE

½ cup all-purpose flour

½ cup brown sugar, packed

1 teaspoon cinnamon

¼ teaspoon salt

½ cup cold salted butter, sliced

Blueberries, raspberries, and strawberries, for serving

Maple syrup, for serving

Preheat oven to 350 degrees F. Using your fingers, spread 2 tablespoons of butter in a 9x13 baking pan, being sure to cover the sides and corners. While your hands are still buttery, tear the bread into bite-sized pieces and spread into the prepared pan.

In a blender, combine the eggs, milk, both sugars, heavy cream, and vanilla extract. Blend until smooth. Pour evenly over the torn bread. Set aside while preparing the crumble or cover and refrigerate overnight.

To prepare the crumble, in a medium bowl, add the flour, brown sugar, cinnamon, salt, and butter. Using a pastry blender, cut the butter into the flour mixture until the butter is the size of small pebbles. Sprinkle the crumble over the French toast. If you are refrigerating the French toast overnight, save the crumble in the refrigerator and add right before baking.

Bake French toast for 50–60 minutes, or until the top is browned. Serve French toast with fresh berries and maple syrup.

french toast roll ups

Is it just mine or do all kids become less picky when they can dip their food into something? I have found that to be a consistent phenomenon. These French toast roll ups can be dipped in maple syrup, making little hands sticky but happy.

ROLL-UPS

2 eggs

¼ cup milk

6 tablespoons salted butter, melted, divided, plus more for frying

3 tablespoons granulated sugar

3 tablespoons brown sugar, packed

1 tablespoon cinnamon

8 slices white bread, crusts removed

SERVING

2 tablespoons granulated sugar

1 teaspoon cinnamon

Maple syrup

In a medium bowl, add the eggs and milk. Whisk well and set aside. In another medium bowl, add 3 tablespoons of the melted butter, the sugar, brown sugar, and cinnamon. Stir and set aside.

Using a rolling pin, flatten each piece of bread to ⅛-inch thick. Spread the butter and sugar mixture onto each slice and roll up.

In a large skillet over medium-high heat, add 3 tablespoons of butter. Once the butter is melted, dip 4 roll ups in the egg and milk mixture and add to the pan. Fry the roll ups, rotating so they brown evenly. Repeat with remaining roll ups, adding more butter as needed for frying.

In a small bowl, combine the sugar and cinnamon. Sprinkle over the top of the finished roll ups and serve with maple syrup for dipping.

fluffy sour cream pancakes

Saturday morning usually means pancakes at our house. Both my husband and I have this recipe practically memorized. It is my favorite go-to basic pancake recipe.

1½ cups all-purpose flour

2 teaspoons baking powder

1 teaspoon baking soda

¼ teaspoon salt

1 cup milk

½ cup sour cream

1 egg

2 tablespoons granulated sugar

1 teaspoon pure vanilla extract

2 tablespoons salted butter, melted

Butter, for cooking

Maple syrup, for serving

KID
FAVORITE

MAKES
4 (4-inch) pancakes or
8 (2-inch) pancakes

TIME
25 minutes

Preheat griddle to medium-high heat.

In a large bowl, add the flour, baking powder, baking soda, and salt. Whisk to combine. In a medium bowl, add the milk, sour cream, egg, sugar, and vanilla extract. Whisk well and then pour into flour mixture. Mix by hand and then fold in the melted butter.

Melt a few tablespoons of butter on the hot griddle. Cook the pancakes ½ cup at a time for 4-inch pancakes or ¼ cup at a time for 2-inch pancakes. Serve with maple syrup.

cranberry coconut granola

Yogurt is so much better with crunchy granola on top. I love this granola with Greek yogurt and sliced bananas or fresh berries. This recipe is great for making it your own. You could switch out the cranberries for another dried fruit—maybe chopped dried apples? Or add some pecans or almonds. You can really do whatever, and it will still be delicious!

Nonstick baking spray

½ cup brown sugar, packed

½ cup honey

¼ cup coconut oil

½ teaspoon salt

½ teaspoon pure vanilla extract

4 cups oats

½ cup shredded coconut

½ cup dried cranberries

Preheat oven to 350 degrees F. Spray a half-sheet baking pan with baking spray and set aside.

In a small saucepan over medium-high heat, add the brown sugar, honey, coconut oil, and salt. Once the brown sugar is dissolved and the coconut oil is melted, stir in the vanilla extract and set aside.

In a large bowl, add the oats, shredded coconut, and cranberries. Stir to combine. Pour the brown sugar mixture over the top. Stir well, being sure everything is well combined. Transfer the granola to the prepared pan. Bake for 10–15 minutes, until lightly browned.

ham and spinach crustless quiche

Brunch is my favorite option for baby showers. I love putting together a really delicious spread with a great variety. This quiche is something I always include and, as a result, I always get asked for the recipe.

Nonstick baking spray

12 eggs

1 cup cottage cheese

1 cup shredded cheddar cheese

1 teaspoon salt

½ teaspoon baking soda

1 cup cubed ham

2 cups chopped fresh spinach

Preheat oven to 350 degrees F. Spray a 9x13 baking pan with baking spray and set aside.

In the bowl of a stand mixer fitted with the whisk attachment, add the eggs, cottage cheese, shredded cheese, salt, and baking soda. Mix on medium speed until well combined. Fold in the ham and spinach by hand.

Pour into the prepared pan. Bake for 25–30 minutes, or until the top is set.

tater tot breakfast casserole

I feel I'm on my A game when I can get a good breakfast into my kids. This tater tot breakfast casserole keeps well in the fridge and heats up fast. When I remember to prepare this early in the week, I'm so glad every morning!

Nonstick baking spray

1 (16-ounce) package pork sausage

5 eggs

1 cup milk

1 teaspoon salt

½ teaspoon ground pepper

2 cups shredded cheddar cheese

1 (32-ounce) package frozen tater tots

Preheat oven to 375 degrees F. Spray a 9x13 baking pan with baking spray and set aside.

In a large skillet over medium-high heat, add the sausage. Sauté, breaking up with a wooden spoon, until cooked through. Spoon the cooked sausage into the prepared pan.

In a medium bowl, add the eggs, milk, salt, and pepper. Whisk well to combine. Stir in the shredded cheese. Pour over the cooked sausage. Add the tater tots on top.

Bake for 45 minutes, until the top is browned.

SOUPS AND SALADS

chicken tortilla soup

Everyone needs a solid chicken tortilla soup recipe in their arsenal. Not only is it easy, but it's liked by everyone. If you are looking for a fun get-together, try a Souper Bowl party. Everyone brings their favorite soup and votes for the best one! This chicken tortilla soup recipe is sure to be a winner.

2 (32-ounce) cartons chicken stock

1 (16-ounce) jar salsa verde

1 rotisserie chicken, shredded, bones and skin discarded

1 (15-ounce) can black beans, drained and rinsed

1 (15-ounce) can pinto beans, drained and rinsed

1 (15-ounce) can corn kernels

1 teaspoon ground cumin

1 teaspoon salt

Shredded cheddar cheese, for serving

Sour cream, for serving

Tortilla strips, for serving

In a large pot over medium-high heat, add chicken stock, salsa verde, shredded chicken, both cans of beans, corn, cumin, and salt. Bring to a boil, then lower the heat to a simmer for 15 minutes.

Serve soup with shredded cheese, sour cream, and tortilla strips as desired.

slow cooker chicken and dumplings

The gnocchi in this recipe are playing the part of dumplings. I like keeping a few packages of prepared gnocchi in my pantry for a quick recipe like this. It's creamy, flavorful, and filling for everyone in your house!

1 (32-ounce) carton chicken stock

½ cup all-purpose flour

2 tablespoons cornstarch

2 teaspoons dried parsley

1 teaspoon salt

1 teaspoon garlic powder

1 teaspoon dried thyme

½ teaspoon dried sage

3 boneless, skinless chicken breasts

½ cup heavy cream

1 (12-ounce) package frozen mixed vegetables

1 (16-ounce) package potato gnocchi

In a slow cooker, add chicken stock, flour, cornstarch, parsley, salt, garlic powder, thyme, and sage. Whisk together until combined. Add chicken breasts. Cook on high for 3–4 hours.

Once cooked, remove the chicken and shred. Add heavy cream, frozen vegetables, gnocchi, and the cooked, shredded chicken to the slow cooker. Stir well. Cook on high one more hour.

your mom's chicken noodle soup

I can always trust recipes from my mom. They are tried and true. If I loved her comforting meals, I know my kids and husband will. Her chicken noodle soup is always just what I need if I'm feeling under the weather.

2 boneless, skinless chicken breasts

4 teaspoons Italian seasoning blend, divided

8 cups water

1½ cups rotini pasta

1 (32-ounce) carton chicken stock

2 carrots, peeled and chopped

2 celery sticks, chopped

1 yellow onion, chopped

2 teaspoons salt

2 teaspoons ground pepper

1 teaspoon garlic salt

In a large pot over high heat, add the chicken breasts, 2 teaspoons Italian seasoning, and water. Bring to a boil, partially cover, and cook until chicken is cooked through or an inserted thermometer reads 165 degrees F. Remove chicken from the water and set aside until cool enough to handle. While chicken cools, add pasta to the boiling water. Cook until pasta is al dente. Set a strainer in a large bowl, remove the cooked pasta and set aside. Pour the water from the bowl back into the large pot and return to the stove. When chicken has cooled, chop into small bite-sized pieces and set aside.

In the same large pot used to cook the chicken and the pasta, to the water add the chicken stock, carrots, celery, onion, salt, pepper, garlic salt, and the remaining 2 teaspoons Italian seasoning. Bring to a boil, then turn down the heat and simmer for 30 minutes. Add in the cooked chicken and pasta and warm before serving.

creamy potato soup

This is my copycat version of a perfect creamy potato soup from a bakery in my hometown. It is all the best things you would have in a baked potato!

1 (30-ounce) bag frozen hash brown potatoes

1 (32-ounce) carton chicken stock

1 (15-ounce) can cream of chicken soup

1 bunch green onion, diced, some reserved for serving

½ cup finely chopped yellow onion

1 teaspoon salt

½ teaspoon ground pepper

6 pieces thick-cut bacon, diced

1 (8-ounce) package cream cheese, softened and roughly chopped

Green onion, chopped, for serving

Bacon bits, for serving

Shredded cheddar cheese, for serving

In a slow cooker, add the hash browns, chicken stock, cream soup, yellow onion, salt, and pepper. Stir well to combine and cook on low for 5–6 hours.

In a small skillet over medium-high heat, add the bacon. Sauté until the bacon is cooked through and crisp, about 10 minutes. Set aside.

A half an hour before serving, add the cream cheese and stir until completely incorporated. Serve soup with green onion, bacon bits, and shredded cheese sprinkled on top.

veggie taco soup

We all need healthy recipes now and then, but it's better if it doesn't feel forced. Veggie taco soup has all the flavor of delicious tacos, but without the guilt.

2 tablespoons extra-virgin olive oil

1 yellow onion, diced

1 teaspoon salt

3 garlic cloves, minced

2 (15-ounce) cans chicken stock

1 (15-ounce) can refried beans

1 (15-ounce) can diced tomatoes

1 (15-ounce) can black beans, drained and rinsed

1 (15-ounce) can great northern beans, drained and rinsed

1 (15-ounce) can corn kernels

1 (4-ounce) can diced green chiles

1 (10-ounce) can diced tomatoes and green chiles, such as Ro-Tel

1 (1-ounce) packet taco seasoning

3 tablespoons lime juice

1 bunch cilantro, chopped

Diced avocado, for serving

1 (9.25-ounce) bag corn chips, such as Fritos, for serving

Shredded cheddar cheese, for serving

Sour cream, for serving

In a large pot over medium heat, add olive oil. Once the oil is heated, add the chopped onion and salt. Sauté for 10 minutes, until softened. Add the garlic and sauté for 1 minute. Add the chicken stock and refried beans and mix until smooth. Next add the diced tomatoes, both kinds of beans, corn, green chiles, Ro-Tel tomatoes, taco seasoning, lime juice, and cilantro. Reduce heat to medium low, cover, and simmer for 30 minutes.

Serve soup with avocado, Fritos, shredded cheese, and sour cream as desired.

bbq chicken chopped salad

I have made this salad since I was a newlywed more than fourteen years ago. It's substantial enough to be a whole meal, with protein, vegetables, and, of course, a little sweetness. I have such sweet memories of early married life with my husband that wash over me when I make this salad for my family.

MAKES
6–8 servings

TIME
45 minutes

8 boneless, skinless chicken tenders

Salt and ground pepper, for seasoning

½ cup barbecue sauce

1 cup frozen corn kernels

2 heads romaine lettuce, chopped

3 Roma tomatoes, diced

3 avocados, diced

1 red onion, diced

1 bunch cilantro, chopped

Lightly crushed tortilla chips, for serving

Ranch dressing, for serving

Preheat a propane grill to medium heat. Season the chicken with salt and pepper on both sides. Grill chicken on both sides until cooked through or an inserted thermometer reads 165 degrees F. Chop the chicken into small, bite-sized pieces and add to a medium bowl. Add barbecue sauce and toss until all the chicken is coated. Set aside.

Add the frozen corn kernels to a small bowl and microwave for 1 minute. Drain any liquid in the bowl and set the corn aside to cool.

In a large salad bowl, add lettuce, tomatoes, avocados, red onion, cilantro, corn, and chicken. Toss and then add crushed tortilla chips and drizzle ranch dressing on top.

wedding shower chicken pasta salad

Food attached to memories always seems to taste better. That is the case for this chicken pasta salad. It was served at my wedding shower many years ago, and is my mom's go-to for special occasions. Lucky for you, you don't have to wait for my mom to make it for you!

SALAD

1 (16-ounce) package farfalle (bow tie) pasta, cooked according to package directions

1 (12.5-ounce) can chunk white chicken breast

1 (10.5-ounce) can mandarin oranges, drained

1 (8-ounce) can pineapple tidbits, drained

1 (8-ounce) can sliced water chestnuts, drained

2 celery sticks, diced

1 bunch green onion, diced

½ cup chopped cashews

½ cup dried cranberries

DRESSING

1 (16-ounce) bottle coleslaw dressing, such as Hidden Valley

1 cup mayonnaise

1 teaspoon salt

1 teaspoon ground pepper

In a large bowl, add the cooked pasta, chicken, mandarin oranges, pineapple, water chestnuts, celery, green onion, cashews, and cranberries.

In a medium bowl, add coleslaw dressing, mayonnaise, salt, and pepper. Whisk to combine and pour over the salad. Toss to combine.

Refrigerate until ready to serve.

cornbread salad

Salad as a meal is my favorite kind of salad. This layered cornbread salad is filled with fresh vegetables, savory ground beef, and a perfect creamy dressing.

SALAD

1 pound ground beef

1 teaspoon salt

1 teaspoon cumin

½ teaspoon oregano

¼ teaspoon chili powder

1 batch Basic Cornbread (see recipe on page 69), crumbled

2 heads romaine lettuce, chopped

1 cup frozen corn kernels, thawed

2 Roma tomatoes, diced

1 (15-ounce) can black beans, drained and rinsed

1 (4-ounce) can sliced black olives, drained

2 cups shredded Mexican blend cheese

1 bunch green onion, sliced

DRESSING

1 cup mayonnaise

1 cup sour cream

1 (1-ounce) packet ranch dressing seasoning, such as Hidden Valley

½ teaspoon garlic powder

½ teaspoon cayenne powder

½ teaspoon paprika

In a large skillet over medium-high heat, add the ground beef, salt, cumin, oregano, and chili powder. Sauté, breaking up the meat with a wooden spoon, until cooked through. Set aside to cool.

In a large glass bowl, layer the cornbread, romaine lettuce, corn, chopped tomato, black beans, cooked ground beef, sliced olives, shredded cheese, and green onion.

In a blender, combine all the dressing ingredients. Blend until smooth and drizzle the dressing on top.

Keep refrigerated until ready to serve.

my favorite pasta salad

There's just no other way to put it: This is my very favorite pasta salad. It's great as a side dish for a summer barbecue. It has my favorite things in it—chunks of cheddar cheese, artichoke hearts, fresh veggies, and a perfectly tangy dressing. You will love this pasta salad as much as I do!

SALAD

1 (7.5-ounce) jar marinated artichoke hearts

1 (16-ounce) package tricolor rotini pasta, cooked according to package directions

1 (7-ounce) package sliced Italian salami, cut into quarters

2 cups cubed cheddar cheese

2 cups chopped fresh broccoli

1 green bell pepper, diced

1 red bell pepper, diced

1 seedless cucumber, diced

1 carrot, peeled and thinly sliced

1 (2.25-ounce) can sliced black olives, drained

¼ cup sliced green onion

DRESSING

½ cup extra-virgin olive oil

¼ cup apple cider vinegar

1 tablespoon lemon pepper seasoning

2 teaspoons granulated sugar

1 teaspoon salt

1 teaspoon dried basil

½ teaspoon dried oregano

Set a strainer over a medium bowl. Drain the artichoke hearts, reserving the liquid. Once the artichoke hearts have drained, roughly chop them and set aside.

In a large bowl, add the cooked pasta, chopped artichoke hearts, salami, cheddar cheese, broccoli, bell peppers, cucumber, carrot, sliced olives, and green onion. Toss well and set aside.

In the medium bowl with the reserved liquid from the artichoke hearts, add all the dressing ingredients and whisk well to combine. Pour over the pasta salad and toss.

MAKES
12 servings

TIME
25 minutes,
plus 4 hours
refrigerated

thanksgiving strawberry pretzel salad

I can't think of a Thanksgiving during my childhood that didn't have this delicious, creamy salad. When I went to Thanksgiving for the first time with my husband's family, I brought this strawberry pretzel salad. It was a huge hit and became a staple at their Thanksgiving table too.

2 cups crushed pretzels

¾ cup salted butter

¾ cup granulated sugar, divided

1 (6-ounce) box strawberry gelatin, such as Jell-O

2 cups boiling water

1 (8-ounce) package cream cheese, softened

1 (8-ounce) tub whipped topping, such as Cool Whip, defrosted

1 (16-ounce) package fresh strawberries, sliced

Preheat oven to 375 degrees F.

In the bowl of a food processor, add the pretzels and process until they are crumbs. In a medium saucepan over medium-high heat, add the butter. Once the butter has melted, remove it from the heat and add 2 tablespoons granulated sugar and the crushed pretzels. Stir well to combine. Pour the pretzel mixture into a 9x13 baking pan and press along the bottom evenly. Bake for 8–10 minutes, until lightly browned. Set aside to cool completely.

In a medium bowl, add the strawberry gelatin and boiling water. Whisk together until the gelatin is dissolved. Set aside to cool (but not set).

In the bowl of a stand mixer fitted with the whisk attachment, add the cream cheese, whipped topping, and remaining sugar. Mix until smooth and well combined. Spread over the cooled pretzel crust, being sure to go completely to the edge. Arrange sliced strawberries over the creamy layer. Pour the cooled gelatin over the strawberries.

Refrigerate for at least 4 hours or up to 1 day before serving.

cowboy caviar salad

We are calling this a salad, but it's also great as a dip. And this recipe makes a ton. So serve some at your next party and then save the rest for dinner the next night!

SALAD

3 Roma tomatoes, diced

2 avocados, diced

1 red onion, diced

1 green bell pepper, diced

1 red bell pepper, diced

1 jalapeño, seeded and diced

1 bunch cilantro, chopped

1 (15-ounce) can black beans, drained and rinsed

1 (15-ounce) can black-eyed peas, drained and rinsed

1 (15-ounce) can corn kernels, drained and rinsed

DRESSING

½ cup extra-virgin olive oil

2 tablespoons lime juice

2 tablespoons red wine vinegar

1 teaspoon granulated sugar

1 teaspoon salt

½ teaspoon ground pepper

¼ teaspoon garlic powder

Tortilla chips, for serving

In a large bowl, add all the salad ingredients. In a jar with a lid, such as a mason jar, add all the dressing ingredients. Seal the jar tightly and shake very well. Pour dressing over the salad and toss to coat. Serve as a salad or serve as a dip with tortilla chips.

feta watermelon salad

It isn't summertime until I'm eating unreasonable amounts of watermelon. Pair it with cheese and I'm a goner. Salty, creamy feta cheese is the best complement to sweet juicy watermelon.

SALAD

5 cups cubed watermelon

1 avocado, diced

1 seedless cucumber, diced

¼ cup thinly sliced red onion

1 (6-ounce) package crumbled feta cheese

⅓ cup mint, torn into small pieces

DRESSING

3 limes, zested and juiced

2 tablespoons extra-virgin olive oil

1 garlic clove, minced

½ teaspoon salt

In a large bowl, add the watermelon, avocado, cucumber, onion, feta cheese, and mint. Toss gently to combine.

In a jar with a lid, such as a mason jar, add the lime juice, zest, olive oil, garlic, and salt. Seal the jar tightly and shake very well. Pour the dressing over the salad and toss to combine.

garden vegetable quinoa salad

I love quinoa! It takes on flavors so well. The dressing in this garden vegetable quinoa salad just makes it. You will love the zing of the lime and the crunchy veggies!

SALAD

⅔ cup dry quinoa, rinsed and cooked according to package directions

1 (10-ounce) carton grape tomatoes, halved

2 avocados, diced

1 yellow bell pepper, diced

1 bunch cilantro, chopped

1 bunch green onions, chopped

DRESSING

3 limes, zested and juiced

¼ cup extra-virgin olive oil

1 tablespoon Dijon mustard

1 teaspoon salt

1 teaspoon ground pepper

In a large bowl, combine the quinoa, grape tomatoes, avocados, bell pepper, cilantro, and green onion. Toss together to combine.

In a jar with a lid, such as a mason jar, add the lime juice, zest, olive oil, Dijon mustard, salt, and pepper. Seal the jar tightly and shake very well.

Pour dressing over the quinoa and vegetables and toss well.

greek salad

My favorite thing about Greek salad is the acidic dressing. It wakes up my tastebuds and keeps me coming back for more. If you have some shredded chicken in the fridge, be sure to add some to this salad!

MAKES
8 servings

TIME
25 minutes

SALAD

2 heads romaine lettuce, chopped

1 (10-ounce) carton grape tomatoes

1 red onion, thinly sliced

1 seedless cucumber, chopped

1 green bell pepper, chopped

1 (15-ounce) can garbanzo beans, drained and rinsed

1 (6-ounce) jar pitted kalamata olives, drained and roughly chopped

1 (6-ounce) package crumbled feta cheese

DRESSING

½ cup extra-virgin olive oil

3 tablespoons red wine vinegar

1 tablespoon lemon juice

1 teaspoon dried oregano

1 teaspoon Dijon mustard

½ teaspoon salt

½ teaspoon ground pepper

1 garlic clove, minced

In a large bowl, add all the salad ingredients. In a jar with a lid, such as a mason jar, add all the dressing ingredients. Seal the jar tightly and shake very well.

When ready to serve, pour dressing over the salad and toss to coat.

MAKES
6 servings

TIME
20 minutes, plus
refrigerated time

herb garden tomato salad

What are your favorite fresh herbs? I love basil the most. And I am not shy with how much I add to this. It is so fresh and bursting with summertime flavor!

1 (16-ounce) carton grape tomatoes, halved

½ red onion, thinly sliced

1 seedless cucumber, diced

Handful of any chopped fresh herbs (such as basil, oregano, dill, parsley, sage, or chives)

3 tablespoons extra-virgin olive oil

1 tablespoon red wine vinegar

½ teaspoon salt

½ teaspoon ground pepper

1 (8-ounce) package mozzarella pearls, drained

Combine all the ingredients in a large bowl and toss well. Refrigerate until ready to serve.

summer party broccoli salad

This is named "Summer Party Broccoli Salad" because it's one of my favorites to serve at summer parties. Everyone, young and old, loves it! I get asked for this recipe so often!

MAKES
6 servings

TIME
45 minutes,
plus 2–3 hours
refrigerated

SALAD

6 strips thick-cut bacon

4 cups fresh broccoli florets, cut into bite-sized pieces

1 cup diced red onion

1 cup sunflower kernels

1 cup dried cranberries

DRESSING

1 cup mayonnaise

½ cup granulated sugar

3 tablespoons apple cider vinegar

1 teaspoon salt

1 teaspoon ground pepper

Preheat oven to 400 degrees F. Add bacon strips to a half-sheet baking pan. Bake for 15–20 minutes, until bacon is crisp. Once it's cool enough to handle, chop the bacon and set aside.

In a large bowl, add the broccoli, cooked bacon, onion, sunflower kernels, and dried cranberries. In a small bowl, add mayonnaise, sugar, vinegar, salt, and pepper. Whisk well to combine. Pour over the broccoli salad and mix well, being sure everything is coated in the dressing.

Refrigerate for 2–3 hours before serving.

LUNCH
AND
DINNER

easy slow cooker
french dip sandwiches

MAKES
6 sandwiches

TIME
20 minutes,
plus 6–8 hours
in the slow cooker

Everyone loves a classic French dip sandwich. This recipes comes together quick in the slow cooker. I like it for those busy weeknights when I have no time to put together a meal. It does take a little advance planning, but it's worth it.

1 (2–3 pound) boneless beef chuck roast

1 (14.5-ounce) can beef broth

1 (10.5-ounce) can beef consommé

1 (10.5-ounce) can French onion soup

1 (6-count) package French sandwich rolls, split

1 (12-ounce) package sliced Swiss cheese

In a slow cooker, add beef roast. Pour broth, consommé, and onion soup over the top. Cook on low for 6–8 hours.

Once cooked, remove the beef roast from the slow cooker. Shred, discarding large pieces of fat, and return the beef to the slow cooker.

To serve, add shredded beef to sandwich rolls and top with Swiss cheese. Serve with individual cups of strained beef au jus from the slow cooker for dipping.

black bean burgers with chipotle sauce

I like to get creative with burger recipes. There is so much you can do besides a basic beef patty, and black bean burgers bring so much flavor to the table! Pair with the chipotle sauce, and you're in business. I would really recommend making a batch of potato wedges or fries to dip in the extra chipotle sauce!

A number of years ago, my dad had some health concerns and his doctor recommended that he switch to a vegan diet. That's heartbreaking for a man who loves a juicy hamburger! In solidarity and support, I decided to go vegan too. I created a number of recipes for my dad that would help him not miss meat so much. This black bean burger was just what the doctor ordered!

SAUCE

1 (7-ounce) can chipotle chiles in adobo sauce (you'll use 2 chipotle chiles, seeds removed, and 1 tablespoon adobo sauce from the can)

1 cup mayonnaise

2 teaspoons lime juice

¼ teaspoon salt

BURGERS

1 green bell pepper, roughly chopped

1 red onion, roughly chopped

2 garlic cloves

1 (15-ounce) can black beans, drained and rinsed

1 egg, beaten

⅔ cup bread crumbs

1 tablespoon chili powder

1 teaspoon cumin

1 teaspoon salt

½ teaspoon ground pepper

2 tablespoons extra-virgin olive oil

SERVING

Hamburger buns

Lettuce leaves

Sliced tomatoes

Sliced avocado

In the bowl of a food processor fitted with the blade attachment, add 2 chipotle chiles, 1 tablespoon adobo sauce, mayonnaise, lime juice, and salt. Process until smooth. Transfer sauce to a small bowl and set aside until serving. Rinse and dry the food processor bowl and blade.

To prepare the patties, add the bell pepper, onion, and garlic to the food processor bowl. Process until smooth and pureed. Transfer mixture to a fine wire mesh strainer over the kitchen sink. Using a rubber scraper, press all the liquid out of the puree. Set aside.

In a large bowl, add the black beans, and mash using a fork or a potato masher. Add the vegetable puree, egg, bread crumbs, chili powder, cumin, salt, and pepper. Mix well. Divide the mixture into 4 equal portions. Shape each portion into a patty. Set aside.

In a large skillet over medium-high heat, add the olive oil. Once the oil is heated, add the black bean patties. Sear on each side until a crust forms, about 5 minutes per side.

Serve patties on hamburger buns with the chipotle sauce, lettuce, tomato, and avocado.

tomato and pesto paninis

Homemade pesto is always delicious, but a jar of prepared pesto is your best friend. You can use it to jazz up all sorts of dishes. Stir into marinara sauce, toss with potatoes before roasting, whisk into a vinaigrette—you just can't go wrong. Here it's used as a sandwich spread. It really takes it to a whole new level!

1½ cups prepared basil pesto, plus more for serving

1 (24-ounce) loaf sourdough bread, sliced

3 Roma tomatoes, thinly sliced

1 (8-ounce) package fresh mozzarella cheese, sliced

Salt and pepper, for seasoning

Salted butter, for cooking

Spread pesto on 12 slices of bread. Lay sliced tomatoes and mozzarella cheese on 6 slices and season with salt and pepper. Top with the remaining bread slices, pesto side down.

Heat a panini pan over medium heat. Melt a few tablespoons of butter on the hot pan. Grill each side of the panini until cheese is melted.

Serve paninis with extra pesto for dipping.

MAKES
6 sandwiches

TIME
25 minutes,
plus 8–10 hours
in the slow cooker

shredded barbecue beef sandwiches

This is how I make everyone happy on Big Game Sunday. I can focus on the fun appetizers while this hit of a recipe works its magic in the slow cooker. Don't have the top sirloin roast called for in this recipe? That's okay! Chuck roast, flank steak, or even stew chunks would work great.

BEEF

1½ cups ketchup

1 cup brown sugar, packed

½ cup apple cider vinegar

2 tablespoons soy sauce

2 tablespoons Worcestershire sauce

1 tablespoon vegetable oil

1 teaspoon garlic powder

1 (3–4 pound) beef top sirloin roast

SAUCE

½ cup mayonnaise

1 teaspoon Dijon mustard

½ teaspoon garlic powder

½ teaspoon Worcestershire sauce

SANDWICHES

6 hamburger buns

In a slow cooker, add ketchup, brown sugar, vinegar, soy sauce, Worcestershire sauce, vegetable oil, and garlic powder. Whisk to combine. Add the beef roast. Using tongs, turn the roast in the sauce, coating all sides. Cook on low for 8–10 hours.

Once cooked, remove the beef roast from the slow cooker. Shred, discarding any large pieces of fat, and return the beef to the slow cooker. Mix with the remaining liquid in the pot.

In a small bowl, add the mayonnaise, mustard, garlic powder, and Worcestershire sauce. Whisk to combine. Spread on hamburger buns and pile on shredded beef.

MAKES
12 sliders

TIME
25 minutes,
plus 8–10 hours
in the slow cooker

teriyaki kalua pork sliders

Hawai'i has my heart. It is one of my favorite places on the planet. Yes, the beaches are great. But the food! The food alone is worth the trip. I particularly love Kalua pork. Smokey, salty, and ready to be put on just about anything. You and yours will love it with teriyaki sauce on top of a soft Hawaiian roll.

1 (4–6 pound) boneless pork shoulder, cut into a few large chunks

3 tablespoons Hawaiian red sea salt

2 tablespoons liquid smoke

3–4 large banana leaves

2 cups teriyaki sauce

1 (12-count) package Hawaiian sweet rolls, such as King's Hawaiian, split

1 (20-ounce) can pineapple slices, drained

In a large bowl, add pork. Sprinkle salt and pour liquid smoke over the top. Using your hands, massage both into the meat.

Line a slow cooker with the banana leaves. Add the pork and fold the banana leaves over the top, covering the pork. Cook on low for 8–10 hours.

Once cooked, shred the meat, discarding any pieces of fat. Remove the banana leaves from the slow cooker and discard. Add the shredded pork and teriyaki to the slow cooker. Stir and set the cooker to warm.

To serve, pile teriyaki pork on a roll and add a slice of pineapple.

blackened salmon tacos with creamy lemon sauce

Putting my favorite foods into tacos is always a win! Blackened salmon, perfectly cooked, in a tortilla with a crunchy slaw and a creamy sauce puts smiles on my family's faces every time. With this recipe, the creamy sauce is doing double duty. It's both what flavors the slaw and what's used on top to finish each taco.

SAUCE

¼ cup mayonnaise

¼ cup sour cream

1 teaspoon lemon juice

2 tablespoons paprika

2 teaspoons brown sugar, packed

2 teaspoons salt

1½ teaspoons garlic powder

1½ teaspoons onion powder

1 teaspoon cayenne pepper

1 teaspoon dried oregano

1 teaspoon dried thyme

SLAW

1 (16-ounce) bag cabbage coleslaw mix

1 bunch cilantro, chopped

SALMON

4 salmon fillet portions, skin removed

2 tablespoons extra-virgin olive oil

12 corn tortillas

In a small bowl, combine the mayonnaise, sour cream, and lemon juice. In another small bowl, combine the paprika, brown sugar, salt, garlic and onion powders, cayenne, oregano, and thyme. Stir together. Reserve 1 tablespoon of the seasoning mix. Add remaining seasoning to the mayonnaise mixture. Whisk well to combine.

In a medium bowl, add the coleslaw mix and cilantro. Pour 2 tablespoons of the mayonnaise mixture over the top and toss well to combine. Set aside. Save the remaining sauce for serving.

Season the salmon fillets with the reserved tablespoon of seasoning mixture. In a large skillet over medium-high heat, add the olive oil. Once the oil is heated, add the salmon fillets, flesh side down. Sear on both sides, until cooked through, about 5 minutes. Transfer salmon to a cutting board and roughly chop into small pieces.

Serve tacos in the corn tortillas with salmon, slaw, and sauce over the top.

cheesy shredded beef tacos

At the moment, it seems birria tacos are a big hit in the food world. It is more simple than you think to make your own version at home. Tender, super flavorful beef is surrounded by stretchy, gooey mozzarella, seared in a skillet and then served with some dipping broth. This will liven up your Taco Tuesdays!

KID
FAVORITE

MAKES
12 tacos

TIME
30 minutes,
plus 8–10 hours
in the slow cooker

TACOS

1 (32-ounce) carton beef stock

¼ cup liquid smoke

1 (4-ounce) can diced green chiles

1 (1-ounce) packet taco seasoning

1 teaspoon salt

1 teaspoon ground pepper

1 teaspoon dried oregano

½ teaspoon cumin

1 (2–3 pound) boneless beef chuck roast

Olive oil, for frying

12 corn tortillas

8 ounces shredded mozzarella cheese

SERVING

1 bunch cilantro, chopped

1 red onion, diced

3 limes, quartered

In a slow cooker, combine beef stock, liquid smoke, green chiles, taco seasoning, salt, pepper, oregano, and cumin. Stir well and add beef chuck roast. Cook on low for 8–10 hours.

Remove beef from the slow cooker. Strain the liquid in the slow cooker, discarding any fat or chile pieces, and reserve the liquid for serving. Shred the beef, removing any fat, and return to the slow cooker.

In a large skillet over medium-high heat, add 2 tablespoons olive oil. Once the oil is heated, add a corn tortilla and a pinch of mozzarella cheese on top. Add shredded meat and fold the tortilla in half. Cook on each side until the tortilla is crisp and the cheese is melted. Repeat with remaining tortillas and cheese.

Serve tacos with a small cup of the cooking liquid for dipping along with chopped cilantro, chopped red onion, and lime wedges.

zesty chicken tacos

I love this easy shredded chicken in tacos, but also on a taco salad, in cheesy enchiladas, or as the feature of gooey nachos. It also freezes really well—so go ahead and make a double batch!

15 ounces chicken stock

½ cup vegetable oil

¼ cup apple cider vinegar

1 (.6-ounce) packet zesty Italian dressing mix, such as Good Seasons

1 tablespoon chili powder

2 teaspoons onion powder

1 teaspoon garlic powder

1 teaspoon paprika

1 teaspoon cumin

1 teaspoon salt

½ teaspoon ground pepper

5 boneless, skinless chicken breasts

1 batch Matt's Guacamole (see recipe on page 203)

1 batch Poolside Pico (see recipe on page 204)

10 flour tortillas, for serving

Shredded iceberg lettuce, for serving

Shredded cheddar cheese, for serving

In a blender, combine the chicken stock; vegetable oil; vinegar; Italian dressing mix; chili, onion, and garlic powders; paprika; cumin; salt; and pepper. Blend until combined.

Add the chicken breasts to a slow cooker. Pour the chicken stock mixture over the chicken. Cook on low for 5–6 hours. Once cooked, remove the chicken and shred. Discard the liquid.

Serve chicken in tortillas topped with lettuce and cheddar cheese.

homemade pizza

I got this recipe from a friend in New Jersey ages ago. I have yet to find a better pizza crust recipe! It works great for a big sheet-pan pizza or for personal pizzas. A batch of this will have you excited for pizza night all over again.

1½ cups warm water (between 100–110 degrees F.)

2½ teaspoons or 1 (¼-ounce) packet active dry yeast

1½ teaspoons brown sugar, packed

1½ teaspoons granulated sugar

1½ teaspoons salt

3½ cups all-purpose flour

Nonstick baking spray

Pizza sauce

Toppings

Shredded mozzarella cheese

In the bowl of a stand mixer fitted with the dough hook attachment, add water, yeast, both sugars, and salt. Using a whisk, mix together until combined. Let sit for 7 minutes. The yeast should create foam on top of the water.

Add the flour, half a cup at a time, while mixing on low speed. Once all the flour is added, mix on low for 5 minutes. Remove the dough from the bowl and spray the bowl with baking spray. Put the dough back in, cover with plastic wrap, and let rise for 30–45 minutes until doubled in size.

Preheat oven to 400 degrees F. Spread risen dough on a half-sheet baking pan. Top with favorite sauce, toppings, and cheese. Bake for 15–20 minutes.

KID FAVORITE

MAKES
enough dough for a half-sheet baking pan pizza or 4 personal pizzas

TIME
45 minutes, plus 45 minutes rising time

MAKES
6 servings

TIME
45 minutes

garlic chicken alfredo

If my Abbi has a request for dinner, you can bet it will be chicken Alfredo. Can you blame her? It has all the best things. Pasta, cheese, cream, chicken: a recipe for a happy tummy.

2 boneless, skinless chicken breasts

1 tablespoon extra-virgin olive oil

Salt and ground pepper, for seasoning

½ cup salted butter

2 cups milk

6 ounces cream cheese

2 garlic cloves, minced

1 teaspoon garlic powder

1 teaspoon Italian seasoning blend

¼ teaspoon salt

¼ teaspoon ground pepper

1 cup grated Parmesan cheese, plus more for serving

1 (16-ounce) package fettuccine pasta, cooked according to package directions

Preheat oven to 425 degrees F. In an 8x8 baking pan, add the chicken. Drizzle olive oil on top and season with salt and pepper. Bake for 25–30 minutes, or until an inserted thermometer reaches 165 degrees F. Once cool enough to handle, slice into strips and set aside.

In a large skillet over medium-high heat, add the butter, milk, and cream cheese. Once melted, add the garlic, garlic powder, Italian seasoning, salt, and pepper. Whisk until combined. When the mixture is simmering, sprinkle in the Parmesan cheese and whisk until smooth.

Add the cooked fettuccine and sliced chicken to the sauce. Mix using tongs. Serve pasta with extra Parmesan cheese on top.

grandma williams's angel chicken pasta

My Grandma Williams was the best cook I have ever known. Time in her kitchen filled my stomach and my heart. When I was twelve years old, I visited her in Idaho for spring break. During that whole week, she would make me anything I wanted, breakfast, lunch, and dinner. I felt like a queen! I not only ate the best food, but I was also able to learn her recipes. A few years later, she had a brain aneurysm and could not cook anymore. I make this pasta dish often, and it always takes me right back to her kitchen.

½ cup apple juice

1 (10.5-ounce) can cream of mushroom soup

1 (8-ounce) package cream cheese, roughly chopped

¼ cup salted butter

1 (.7-ounce) packet Italian dressing mix, such as Good Seasons

1 teaspoon salt

6 boneless, skinless chicken breasts

1 (16-ounce) package angel hair pasta, cooked according to package directions

1 bunch green onion, chopped

In a medium saucepan over medium-high heat, add the apple juice, cream of mushroom soup, cream cheese, butter, Italian dressing mix, and salt. Cook, stirring often, until the cream cheese is melted. Add the chicken breasts to the slow cooker and pour the creamy mixture over the top. Cook on low for 5–6 hours.

Serve chicken over angel hair pasta and garnish with green onion.

LUNCH AND DINNER

creamy bolognese with angel hair pasta

Here is one of my fast dinner secrets: Use angel hair pasta. It boils up quickly and gets dinner on the table lickety-split. Pair it with this hearty sauce and it's not only speedy, but filling as well.

KID FAVORITE

MAKES
6 servings

TIME
35 minutes

2 tablespoons extra-virgin olive oil

1 (1-pound) package ground turkey

½ red onion, diced

½ green bell pepper, diced

1 teaspoon salt

2 (15-ounce) cans tomato sauce

2 teaspoons Italian seasoning blend

½ teaspoon fennel seeds

¼ teaspoon crushed red pepper flakes

½ cup heavy cream

1 (16-ounce) package angel hair pasta, cooked according to package directions

In a large skillet, over medium-high heat, add the olive oil. Once the oil is heated, add the ground turkey, onion, bell pepper, and salt. Sauté, breaking up the ground turkey with a wooden spoon, until cooked through. Reduce heat to low and stir in the tomato sauce, Italian seasoning, fennel seeds, red pepper flakes, and heavy cream. Simmer for 15 minutes.

Serve sauce over the cooked pasta.

MAKES
8–12 servings

TIME
45 minutes

mac and cheese

What is it is about homemade mac and cheese that feels so comforting? Boxed mac and cheese has its place, but the good homemade stuff is more flavorful and filling—and that breadcrumb crust on top is just right.

Nonstick baking spray

¾ cup salted butter, divided

6 tablespoons all-purpose flour

4½ cups milk

4 cups shredded cheddar cheese

1 teaspoon ground mustard

1 teaspoon salt

1 teaspoon ground pepper

1 (16-ounce) package elbow macaroni, cooked according to package directions

1 (15-ounce) package bread crumbs

Preheat the oven to 375 degrees F. Spray a 9x13 baking pan with baking spray.

In a large pot over medium-high heat, add ½ cup butter. Once the butter has melted, add the flour and whisk until combined. Pour in the milk and stir constantly until the mixture begins to bubble and thicken. Sprinkle in the shredded cheese and stir until melted. Add the ground mustard, salt, and pepper. Add the cooked macaroni, mix well, and pour into the prepared pan.

In a medium bowl, add the remaining ¼ cup butter and melt in the microwave in 10-second increments. Once melted, stir in the bread crumbs and then sprinkle over the macaroni. Bake for 35–40 minutes, or until the top is browned.

classic lasagna

This is the lasagna of my childhood. My mom's recipe is the one I make for my own kids. Not only is it nostalgic, it is delicious and simple, which is why I call it a classic!

2 tablespoons extra-virgin olive oil

1 (1-pound) package ground beef

1 teaspoon salt

1 teaspoon ground pepper

2 (15-ounce) cans tomato sauce

1 teaspoon dried basil

1 teaspoon dried oregano

1 (16-ounce) box lasagna noodles, cooked according to package directions

1 (16-ounce) tub cottage cheese

1 (8-ounce) bag shredded Parmesan cheese

1 (8-ounce) bag shredded mozzarella cheese

Preheat oven to 375 degrees F.

In a large skillet over medium-high heat, add the olive oil. Once the oil is heated, add the ground beef, salt, and pepper. Sauté, breaking up the meat with a wooden spoon, until cooked through, about 10 minutes. Add the tomato sauce, basil, and oregano. Reduce heat to medium and simmer for 10 minutes.

In a 9x13 baking pan, begin building the lasagna. Add 1 cup of the sauce mixture and spread evenly. Layer on half the cooked noodles, half the cottage cheese and half the Parmesan cheese. For the final layer, spread half the remaining sauce mixture over the Parmesan cheese. Then layer the remaining cooked noodles, remaining cottage cheese, remaining Parmesan cheese, and the rest of the sauce mixture. Finish with the shredded mozzarella on top.

Place the 9x13 pan on a half-sheet baking pan to catch any drips. Bake for 45–50 minutes, until the cheese is browned and the lasagna is bubbling. Let sit for at least 15 minutes after baking so the sauce and cheese have a chance to set.

new jersey chicken lasagna

MAKES
8–12 servings

TIME
60 minutes

Sometimes a recipe is much more than a list of ingredients. This one is near and dear to my heart. It reminds me of the people I knew and loved in New Jersey when I lived there so many years ago. I cannot count how many times I've made this. It's my favorite dish to bring to someone after they have had a baby. It's just plain good. I have been asked for this recipe so many times, it only makes sense to put it in this book!

1 (16-ounce) package lasagna noodles

1 (10.5-ounce) can cream of chicken soup

1 (10.5-ounce) can cream of
   mushroom soup

1 cup cottage cheese

¾ cup shredded Parmesan cheese

½ cup sour cream

¼ cup chopped green onion,
   plus more for garnish

1 teaspoon salt

½ teaspoon ground pepper

¼ teaspoon dried basil

¼ teaspoon dried oregano

1 rotisserie chicken, shredded,
   bones and skin discarded

Nonstick baking spray

1 cup shredded cheddar cheese

1 cup shredded mozzarella cheese

Preheat oven to 375 degrees F.

Bring a large pot of water to boil. Once boiling, cook the lasagna noodles according to the package directions. Drain and set aside.

In the bowl of a stand mixer fitted with the paddle attachment, add both cream soups, the cottage cheese, Parmesan cheese, sour cream, green onion, salt, pepper, basil, oregano, and chicken. Mix on medium speed until well combined.

Spray a 9x13 baking pan with baking spray, then add half the noodles, half the chicken mixture, then the cheddar cheese. Add the remaining noodles, remaining chicken mixture, then the mozzarella cheese.

Bake for 40–45 minutes. Garnish with green onion before serving.

MAKES
6 servings

TIME
35 minutes

baked spinach and sausage gnocchi

Here is my favorite way to sneak some spinach into my kids—cover it in carbs and cheese. Before they know what is happening, they have licked their plates.

1 (16-ounce) package potato gnocchi

3 tablespoons extra-virgin olive oil, divided

2 teaspoons salt, divided

1½ cups loosely packed fresh baby spinach

1 (1-pound) package mild Italian sausage

1 (8-ounce) carton white mushrooms, sliced

1 teaspoon ground pepper

2 tablespoons salted butter

1 garlic clove, minced

2 tablespoons all-purpose flour

1½ cups whole milk

1 (15-ounce) can chicken stock

½ cup grated Parmesan cheese

Preheat the oven to 425 degrees F.

Fill a large saucepan ¾ full of water, and add 1 tablespoon olive oil and 1 teaspoon salt. Bring to a boil, and cook the gnocchi according to package instructions. Just before the gnocchi is done, add the spinach and allow to wilt. Drain the gnocchi and spinach and set aside.

In a large ovenproof skillet over medium-high heat, add the sausage. Sauté, breaking up the sausage with a wooden spoon, until cooked through, about 10 minutes. Using a slotted spoon, transfer to a plate and set aside.

In the same skillet over medium-high heat, add the remaining olive oil. Once the oil is hot, add the mushrooms, the remaining salt, and pepper. Sauté until lightly browned, about 10 minutes. Add the butter. When the butter has melted, add the garlic and then sprinkle the flour over the top and sauté until the flour is absorbed and the flour smell is gone, about 3 minutes. Pour in milk and chicken stock. Stir until the mixture begins to thicken.

Once the sauce is thickening, add the cooked gnocchi and spinach. Stir well. Sprinkle Parmesan cheese on top. Transfer skillet to the oven, and bake for 20–25 minutes, until the top is golden brown.

beef and biscuit pot pie

It doesn't get super cold where I live in Southern California—a rainy day is as close to winter weather as we get. But that doesn't mean I'm not going to make some of my favorite comfort foods. This take on pot pie tastes even better when wearing a hoodie and comfy socks.

BEEF

2 tablespoons extra-virgin olive oil

1 (1-pound) package ground beef

1 teaspoon salt

1 teaspoon ground pepper

2 cups beef stock

1 (16-ounce) bag frozen mixed vegetables

1 (8-ounce) package cream cheese, roughly chopped

1 teaspoon dried thyme

1 teaspoon dried sage

BISCUITS

2½ cups all-purpose flour

2 tablespoons baking powder

1 teaspoon granulated sugar

1 teaspoon salt

½ cup cold salted butter, sliced

1 cup milk, plus more for brushing

In an ovenproof skillet over medium-high heat, add the olive oil. Once the oil is heated, add the ground beef and season with salt and pepper. Sauté, stirring often, until the beef is cooked through. Remove beef to a separate bowl.

Lower heat to medium. Add the beef stock, frozen vegetables, cream cheese, thyme, and sage. Bring to a simmer and stir until the cream cheese is melted. Add the cooked ground beef. Reduce the heat to low and simmer while preparing the biscuits.

Preheat oven to 425 degrees F. For the biscuits, add flour, baking powder, sugar, and salt to a large bowl and whisk until well blended. Add cold sliced butter. Using a pastry blender, cut the butter into the flour mixture until the butter is the size of small pebbles. Stir in the milk with a wooden spoon until a dough forms. On a floured surface, turn out the dough and pat into a 1-inch-thick circle. Cut out circles using a biscuit cutter or a small drinking glass.

Once all the biscuits are cut out, set them on top of the beef mixture. Pour a small amount of milk into a bowl and, using a pastry brush, brush milk on top of each biscuit.

Bake for 10–12 minutes, or until the biscuits are browned.

beef enchilada casserole

There are a few recipes that are my go-tos for taking to families that need a meal, such as someone with a new baby, someone who's sick, or someone who just needs a boost. This enchilada casserole is one of them. I also love subbing in shredded chicken for the ground beef.

1 (1-pound) package ground beef

1 teaspoon salt

1 teaspoon ground pepper

1 teaspoon onion powder

½ teaspoon garlic powder

½ teaspoon chili powder

1 (15-ounce) can corn kernels, drained

2 (15-ounce) cans tomato sauce

12 corn tortillas, cut in half

4 cups shredded Mexican cheese blend, divided

1 (2.25-ounce) can sliced black olives, divided

½ cup chopped green onion

Sour cream, for serving

KID FAVORITE

MAKES
8 servings

TIME
45 minutes

Preheat oven to 400 degrees F.

In a large skillet over medium-high heat, add the ground beef, salt, pepper, and the onion, garlic, and chili powders. Sauté, breaking up the ground beef with wooden spoon, until cooked through. Remove the pan from the heat and stir in the corn and tomato sauce.

In a 9x13 pan, add a small amount of tomato sauce mixture, just to cover the bottom. Line the bottom of the pan with 10 tortilla halves, cut side facing outward, then add two halves in the middle to fully cover the pan. Spread half the remaining tomato sauce mixture over the tortillas. Sprinkle 2 cups of the shredded cheese and half of the sliced black olives over the tomato sauce. Repeat the layers of tortillas, tomato sauce mixture, cheese, and olives.

Bake for 30–35 minutes, or until the top is browned. Sprinkle green onion on top. Serve with a dollop of sour cream.

LUNCH AND DINNER

buffalo chicken pizza

I *love* buffalo chicken dip. You know the one—creamy, tangy, a little spicy. I love it so much, I made it into a pizza! You won't be able to have just one piece.

3 boneless, skinless chicken breasts

Extra-virgin olive oil

Salt and ground pepper, for seasoning

1 batch homemade pizza dough
  (see recipe on page 147)

1 (8-ounce) package cream
  cheese, softened

½ cup ranch dressing, such
  as Hidden Valley

⅓ cup hot sauce, such as Frank's
  Red Hot, plus more for garnish

1 cup shredded cheddar cheese, divided

2 cups shredded mozzarella cheese

1 bunch green onions, chopped

Preheat oven to 425 degrees F. Place the chicken breasts on a half-sheet baking pan. Drizzle olive oil on top and season with salt and pepper. Roast for 25–30 minutes, or until an inserted thermometer reaches 165 degrees F. Once cool enough to handle, shred the chicken and set aside.

On another half-sheet baking pan, stretch the pizza dough to the edges and set aside.

In the bowl of a stand mixer fitted with the whisk attachment, add cream cheese, ranch dressing, ⅓ cup Frank's Red Hot sauce, and ½ cup cheddar cheese. Mix until smooth and well combined. Spread the cream cheese mixture over the pizza dough, leaving the edges bare so there is a crust. Add the shredded chicken evenly across the cream cheese mixture. Sprinkle the remaining ½ cup of cheddar cheese and the mozzarella over the chicken.

Bake for 15–20 minutes, until the cheese is melted and browned. Before serving, add green onions on top and drizzle with more Frank's Red Hot sauce.

chicken fajita bowls

All the best parts of chicken fajitas, but way easier to eat! I love taking a recipe that can be tricky for little hands to eat and turning it into a bowl. The chicken and vegetables also freeze great, so maybe make a double batch to have an extra meal on hand.

2 tablespoons extra-virgin olive oil

1 green bell pepper, thinly sliced

1 red bell pepper, thinly sliced

1 red onion, thinly sliced

1 teaspoon salt

3 boneless, skinless chicken breasts, cut into small, bite-sized pieces

1 (15-ounce) can black beans, drained and rinsed

3 garlic cloves, minced

1 (1.25-ounce) packet fajita seasoning

1 bunch cilantro, chopped

Cooked white rice, for serving

1 avocado, chopped, for serving

In a large skillet over medium-high heat, add olive oil. Once the oil is heated, add the bell peppers, red onion, and salt. Sauté until the vegetables are softened and charred, about 15 minutes.

Reduce heat to medium. Add the chicken, beans, and garlic. Sprinkle the fajita seasoning on top. Then fill the packet with water and empty into the pan. Stir well, until the chicken and vegetables are coated in the seasoning. Cover the skillet and cook for 10 minutes, stirring occasionally, until a thermometer inserted into a piece of chicken reads 165 degrees F. Stir in the chopped cilantro.

Serve chicken fajitas in bowls over white rice and garnish with chopped avocado.

MAKES
6 servings

TIME
20 minutes,
plus 4–6 hours
in the slow cooker

creamy chicken and broccoli

I have yet to find a child who won't eat their broccoli when it comes paired with chicken and a creamy sauce. Really though, a picky child or a picky adult can be happy with a dish like this.

1 (15-ounce) can chicken stock

1 (10.5-ounce) can cream of chicken soup

1 (10.5-ounce) can cream of
   mushroom soup

1 cup shredded cheddar cheese

¾ cup sour cream

1 tablespoon salt

1 tablespoon ground pepper

4 boneless, skinless chicken breasts

1 (12-ounce) bag frozen broccoli florets

Cooked white rice, for serving

In a slow cooker, add the chicken stock, both cream soups, cheddar cheese, sour cream, salt, and pepper. Mix together until smooth and well combined. Add chicken breasts. Cook on low for 4–6 hours.

Once cooked, remove the chicken and shred with a fork. Return shredded chicken to the slow cooker and add the frozen broccoli. Gently mix together. Cook on low for an additional 10 minutes.

Serve over cooked rice.

matt's guacamole-stuffed chicken

MAKES
6 servings

TIME
45 minutes

My husband is many things, but a chef he is not—except for this amazing creation! He stuffs his own guacamole recipe into a chicken breast, wraps it in bacon, and bakes it in the oven. You would never know this is his only crack at writing a recipe!

Nonstick baking spray

6 boneless, skinless chicken breasts

Salt, pepper, and lemon pepper seasoning blend, for seasoning

1 batch Matt's Guacamole (see recipe on page 203)

6 slices thick-cut bacon

8 ounces shredded Monterey Jack cheese

Sour cream, for serving

1 batch Poolside Pico (see recipe on page 204), for serving

Preheat oven to 375 degrees F. Spray a 9x13 baking pan with baking spray.

Using a sharp knife, slice a pocket into the side of each chicken breast, being sure to not cut all the way through to the other side. Season each chicken breast with salt, pepper, and lemon pepper seasoning, including inside the pocket.

Fill each pocket with a heaping tablespoon of guacamole. Wrap a piece of bacon around the chicken and secure with toothpicks.

Place each filled and wrapped chicken breast in the prepared baking pan. Sprinkle shredded cheese on top. Bake for 35–40 minutes, or until an inserted thermometer reads 165 degrees F.

Remove toothpicks and serve with sour cream and Poolside Pico.

slow cooker hawaiian haystacks

Ever had a meal that just tastes and feels like childhood? This one is at the top of the list for me! I have so many good memories of this meal being comforting and familiar. Creamy chicken and crunchy toppings in every bite makes it the ultimate in memorable meals.

2 boneless, skinless chicken breasts

½ cup salted butter

½ cup all-purpose flour

1 teaspoon salt

½ cup sour cream

1 (32-ounce) carton chicken stock

2 teaspoons ranch seasoning, such as Hidden Valley

¼ teaspoon garlic salt

Cooked rice, for serving

TOPPING OPTIONS

Chow mein noodles

Sliced almonds

Pineapple tidbits

Shredded coconut

Diced tomatoes

Diced avocado

Chopped green onion

Sliced black olives

In a slow cooker set to low, add chicken.

In a small sauce pot over medium-high heat, add butter. Once the butter has melted, stir in the flour, salt, sour cream, chicken stock, ranch seasoning, and garlic salt. Whisk to combine. Pour over the chicken in the slow cooker. Cook on low for 4–6 hours.

Once the chicken is cooked, remove from the slow cooker and set aside until cool enough to handle. Shred and put the chicken back into the slow cooker and mix it into the sauce.

Serve chicken mixture over cooked rice with preferred toppings.

slow cooker ranch chicken baked potatoes

MAKES
6 servings

TIME
20 minutes,
plus 5–6 hours
in the slow cooker

You are going to love this recipe. Besides it being delicious and easy, it's efficient too! We cook the baked potatoes on top of the chicken in the slow cooker. You can truly set it and forget it!

5 boneless, skinless chicken breasts

1 (8-ounce) package cream cheese, cut into chunks

1 (1-ounce) packet ranch seasoning, such as Hidden Valley

6 russet potatoes, pierced and wrapped tightly in foil

6 strips thick-cut bacon, diced

In a slow cooker, add the chicken and cream cheese. Sprinkle the ranch seasoning over the top. Lay a large piece of foil over the top. On top of the foil, add the wrapped potatoes, packing the slow cooker tightly if needed. Cook on low for 5–6 hours.

While the chicken and potatoes cook, prepare the bacon. In a skillet over medium-high heat, add the diced bacon. Cook, stirring frequently, until the bacon is crisp. Remove from heat and set aside.

Once the chicken and potatoes are cooked, carefully remove the potatoes and set aside. Discard the foil covering the chicken. Using two forks, shred the chicken into bite-sized pieces and stir to combine. Pour the cooked bacon and rendered fat into the chicken mixture and fold in with a rubber scraper.

Split the baked potatoes and add a big scoop of the bacon ranch chicken to each potato.

TIME
20 minutes,
plus about 14 hours
in the slow cooker

sweet pork nachos

What is a meal you can eat over and over and never get sick of it? For me, it's nachos. I will never tire of the salty, cheesy, crunchy hit of nachos. Add sweet pork as in this recipe, and I'm in heaven!

SWEET PORK

3–4 pounds pork shoulder roast

1 (20-ounce) bottle of cola, such as Dr Pepper

2 cups brown sugar, packed

1 (15-ounce) can diced tomatoes

1 (8-ounce) can diced green chiles

1 teaspoon salt

1 teaspoon onion powder

1 teaspoon garlic powder

½ teaspoon chili powder

QUESO

1 (16-ounce) package cheese, such as Velveeta, roughly chopped

1 cup milk

1 (1-ounce) packet taco seasoning

NACHOS

1 (16-ounce) bag tortilla chips, divided

1 (15-ounce) can black beans, drained and rinsed, divided

1 (32-ounce) bag shredded Mexican blend cheese, divided

1 batch Matt's Guacamole (see recipe on page 203)

1 batch Poolside Pico (see recipe on page 204)

In a slow cooker, add the pork shoulder. Add enough water to come halfway up the pot. Cook on low heat overnight, or for at least 8 hours.

Once cooked, remove the pork from the slow cooker. Discard liquid, bone, and any remaining fat. In the bottom of the pot, add Dr Pepper, brown sugar, diced tomatoes, diced green chiles, salt, and the onion, garlic, and chili powders. Stir together. Add the pork back into the slow cooker and coat it in the sauce. Cook on low for an additional 6 hours.

Remove pork from the slow cooker. Shred the pork, removing any fat, and return to the slow cooker. Set heat to warm.

In a medium saucepan, add all queso ingredients. Stir often, until the cheese is melted and the mixture is smooth.

Preheat the oven to 425 degrees F. Using a half-sheet baking pan, build the nachos. Layer half of each the tortilla chips, queso, shredded pork, black beans, and shredded cheese. Repeat with the remaining ingredients.

Bake nachos for 30 minutes, until the cheese is melted and the chips are lightly browned. Serve nachos with Matt's Guacamole and Poolside Pico.

SIDES AND DIPS

cashew bacon green beans

My good friend Kelly is an amazing chef and is always inspiring me to try new things. These green beans are such a crowd pleaser. I would never think to add cashews to green beans, but it completely works!

6 strips thick-cut bacon, cut into ½-inch pieces

2 pounds fresh green beans

1 cup salted cashews

2 cloves garlic, minced

2 tablespoons extra-virgin olive oil

1 teaspoon salt

Preheat the oven to 450 degrees F. In a skillet over medium-high heat, add the bacon. Cook until the bacon has rendered some fat, but is still undercooked. Set aside.

On a half-sheet baking pan, add the green beans, cashews, garlic, olive oil, salt, and partially cooked bacon. Toss together until everything is coated in olive oil. Roast for 20 minutes, flip with a spatula, then roast for 10 more minutes.

SIDES AND DIPS

yummy potatoes

It would be disrespectful to my family heritage to not make funeral potatoes. Luckily, my whole family loves them—if they didn't, I'd be concerned. Cheddar cheese, potatoes, and a crunchy topping make for an ultimately delicious comfort food!

1 (30-ounce) bag frozen
   hashbrown potatoes

2 (10.5-ounce) cans cream
   of chicken soup

2 cups shredded cheddar cheese

2 cups sour cream

1 bunch green onions, chopped,
   some reserved for serving

1 teaspoon salt

1 teaspoon ground pepper

3 cups corn flakes cereal,
   such as Kellogg's

½ cup salted butter, melted

Preheat oven to 375 degrees F.

In a large bowl, add the potatoes, cream soup, shredded cheese, sour cream, green onion, salt, and pepper. Mix well, being sure all ingredients are combined. Pour into a 9x13 baking pan and spread evenly.

In the mixing bowl, add the corn flakes and crush roughly with your hands. Pour the melted butter over the top and mix well. Spread the corn flake mixture over the potatoes evenly.

Bake for 45 minutes, until the top is lightly browned. Top with the reserved green onion before serving.

uncle todd's mashed potatoes

My dad grew up in Idaho with four brothers. As you can imagine, it was a rough and tumble time! Their household was a meat-and-potatoes kind of place. My dad's brother Todd took regular mashed potatoes and made them into something special. Uncle Todd's method is the only way to go! Make them and you will see why!

8 medium-sized Yukon gold potatoes, diced

2 cups heavy cream

2 cups whole milk

4 garlic cloves, smashed

4 sprigs fresh thyme

1 bay leaf

2 tablespoons salted butter

1 tablespoon extra-virgin olive oil

1 teaspoon ground mustard

Salt and pepper, for seasoning

In a large pot over high heat, add the potatoes, cream, milk, garlic, thyme, and bay leaf. Boil for 10 minutes, or until the potatoes are easily pierced by a fork. Drain the potatoes, but reserve the liquid. Discard the thyme and bay leaf.

Transfer the potatoes to a large bowl. Using a potato masher, mash the potatoes until smooth. Add butter, olive oil, and ground mustard. Gradually fold in the boiling liquid until desired consistency. Season with salt and pepper to taste.

grandma schofield's sweet potatoes

Thanksgiving with my Grandma Schofield would always include her famous sweet potatoes. They are different from any others I've tried. The secret to them is the tart Granny Smith apples. Even though she passed when I was a teen, Grandma Schofield still feels close when this dish is on the table.

6 sweet potatoes or yams, peeled and chopped

6 Granny Smith apples, peeled and chopped

3 cups water

1½ cups granulated sugar

1 cup salted butter

¼ cup cornstarch

1½ teaspoons salt

¼ teaspoon cinnamon

Bring a large pot of water to boil over high heat. Once boiling, add the sweet potatoes. Boil for 10 minutes, or until easily pierced by a fork. Drain the sweet potatoes and transfer to a 9x13 baking pan. Add the chopped apples and toss to combine.

Preheat oven to 350 degrees F. In a medium saucepan over medium-high heat, add the water, sugar, butter, cornstarch, salt, and cinnamon. Bring to a simmer, stirring often. Once the sugar is dissolved and the butter is melted, pour over the top of the sweet potatoes and apples.

Bake for 40–45 minutes, until the apples are soft and the top is browned.

glazed rainbow carrots

Next time you are assigned a side dish for a family gathering or a potluck dinner, bring these gorgeous carrots. They're a mixture of color, texture, and taste that is sure to wow.

2 pounds rainbow carrots, peeled and sliced into ½-inch coins

2 tablespoons brown sugar, packed

2 tablespoons extra-virgin olive oil

2 tablespoons pure maple syrup

1 teaspoon salt

½ teaspoon ground pepper

1 (8-ounce) package pomegranate seeds

½ cup chopped pistachios

¼ cup crumbled feta cheese

Preheat oven to 375 degrees F. Add the carrots to a half-sheet baking pan.

In a small bowl, add the brown sugar, olive oil, maple syrup, salt, and pepper. Whisk to combine. Pour over the carrots and toss to coat. Roast the carrots for 35–40 minutes, until they are softened and browned.

Transfer the carrots to a serving dish. Sprinkle pomegranate seeds, pistachios, and feta cheese on top.

SIDES AND DIPS

parmesan creamed corn

My creamed corn recipe is sure to satisfy. I use bacon and Parmesan to bring maximum mouthwatering flavor. This creamed corn is great as a side dish next to grilled burgers or homemade macaroni and cheese (see recipes for Black Bean Burgers with Chipotle Sauce on page 132 or Mac and Cheese on page 154).

6 slices thick-cut bacon, cut into ¼-inch pieces

1 yellow onion, diced

1 teaspoon salt

1 teaspoon ground pepper

2 tablespoons all-purpose flour

2 cups whole milk

½ cup grated Parmesan cheese

5 cups frozen corn kernels

¼ cup chopped chives

In a large skillet over medium-high heat, add the bacon. Cook until browned and crisp. Transfer with a slotted spoon to a small bowl, leaving the rendered fat in the pan.

Return the pan to the heat and reduce the heat to medium. Add the onion, salt, and pepper. Sauté until onion is softened, about 10 minutes. Sprinkle the flour over the top and sauté until flour is absorbed, about 2 minutes. Pour in the milk and stir until thickened. Sprinkle the Parmesan cheese over the top. Once the cheese is melted, add the corn. Cook for an additional 3 minutes. Stir in the bacon and chives.

cilantro lime rice

If you make a lot of Mexican food at your house, you have to have a recipe for cilantro lime rice! It goes perfectly with everything from tacos to burritos to salad. And the leftovers are delicious in Chicken Tortilla Soup (see recipe on page 97).

4 cups water

2 cups basmati rice

2 teaspoons salt

3 tablespoons extra-virgin
   olive oil, divided

1 lime, juiced

2 tablespoons granulated sugar

⅓ cup chopped cilantro

In a medium saucepan over high heat, add the water, rice, salt, and 1 tablespoon olive oil. Bring to a boil, reduce heat to medium-low and cover. Cook until the rice has absorbed the liquid and is tender.

In a small bowl, add the remaining 2 tablespoons olive oil, lime juice, sugar, and cilantro. Stir to combine. Pour over the cooked rice and stir.

SIDES AND DIPS

seven-layer dip

A quick flip through my cookbook and you will see that I am a big fan of dips! I just have so many dip recipes I love! This classic seven-layer dip with chips might be my ultimate favorite! You will love this recipe!

MAKES
12 servings

TIME
25 minutes

1 (1-ounce) packet taco seasoning

1 (16-ounce) tub sour cream

1 (15-ounce) can refried beans

1 batch Matt's Guacamole (see recipe on page 203)

2 cups shredded Mexican cheese blend

1 (2.25-ounce) can sliced olives

3 Roma tomatoes, diced

1 bunch green onions, chopped

Tortilla chips, for serving

Add the taco seasoning to the sour cream and whisk until combined and set aside.

In a 9x13 baking pan, layer the ingredients as follows:
- Refried beans
- Sour cream
- Guacamole
- Shredded cheese
- Sliced olives
- Diced tomatoes
- Chopped green onion

Cover with plastic wrap and refrigerate until ready to serve. Eat with tortilla chips.

SIDES AND DIPS

197

creamy green chile corn dip

Both my husband and I love anything with green chiles. So a creamy dip filled with green chiles is a no-brainer. Have leftover dip? Try substituting it for the guacamole in Matt's Guacamole-Stuffed Chicken (see recipe on page 173)!

MAKES
8 servings

TIME
25 minutes

2 cups shredded Mexican blend cheese

1 cup mayonnaise

1 cup sour cream

1 teaspoon salt

¼ teaspoon ground pepper

¼ teaspoon garlic powder

3 cups frozen corn kernels

1 (4-ounce) can mild chopped green chiles

1 (4-ounce) can mild chopped jalapeños

1 (2.25-ounce) can sliced black olives

¼ cup chopped green onions

Tortilla chips or crackers, for serving

In the bowl of a stand mixer fitted with the paddle attachment, add the shredded cheese, mayonnaise, sour cream, salt, pepper, and garlic powder. Mix on medium speed until well combined. Add the corn, green chiles, jalapeños, black olives, and green onions and mix on low speed until combined.

Transfer to a medium bowl and refrigerate for at least 2 hours. Serve with chips or crackers.

jalapeño popper dip

Who doesn't love a good jalapeño popper? I know I sure do! Made into a dip, it's almost better than the real thing. There's plenty of gooey cheese and the right amount of spice. With this recipe, my favorite dippers are pretzel crackers!

2 (8-ounce) packages cream cheese, softened

1 cup mayonnaise

1 cup shredded Mexican blend cheese

1 cup shredded Parmesan cheese

1 (4-ounce) can diced jalapeño

1 (4-ounce) can diced green chiles

½ teaspoon salt

½ teaspoon ground pepper

1 cup bread crumbs

¼ cup salted butter, melted

Pretzel crackers, for dipping

Preheat oven to 375 degrees F. In the bowl of a stand mixer fitted with the paddle attachment, add the cream cheese, mayonnaise, both cheeses, jalapeños, green chiles, salt, and pepper. Mix on medium speed until well combined. Transfer to a 8x8 baking pan.

In a small bowl, combine the bread crumbs and melted butter. Stir well and spread over the dip. Bake for 20 minutes until the top is browned. Serve with pretzel crackers.

matt's guacamole

No one makes better guacamole than my husband. It has become famous in our family. Everyone expects it to be at every gathering, party, holiday, or hangout. The whole issue of guacamole turning brown? That's never a problem because there isn't ever any left!

MAKES
6 servings

TIME
20 minutes

3 avocados, chopped

3 tablespoons finely chopped cilantro

3 tablespoons finely diced red onion

1 lime, juiced

1 teaspoon lemon pepper seasoning

1 teaspoon ground pepper

1 teaspoon salt

1 Roma tomato, chopped

Tortilla chips, for serving

   In a medium bowl, add the avocado, cilantro, onion, lime juice, lemon pepper, pepper, and salt. Mix together until combined. Mash with a potato masher if you want a smoother guacamole. Stir in the tomatoes. Eat with tortilla chips.

poolside pico

If it's summer, then I'm making this all the time. And it's called poolside pico for a reason—I love bringing it to pool parties. If I'm sitting with friends while our kids splash and swim, poolside pico is the best snack.

10 Roma tomatoes, chopped

1 red onion, finely diced

4 garlic cloves, minced

1 bunch cilantro, finely chopped

2 teaspoons salt

2 limes, juiced

Tortilla chips, for scooping

    In a large bowl, add the tomatoes, red onion, garlic, cilantro, salt, and lime juice. Stir together and serve with tortilla chips.

SIDES AND DIPS

garden salsa

I don't claim to be a professional gardener, but I do have a spot in my backyard to grow some of my favorite veggies—and they make the best fresh salsa! This recipe makes plenty, so you can have some in the fridge ready to go anytime.

2 pounds tomatoes, roughly chopped

1 bunch cilantro, roughly chopped

1 bunch green onion, roughly chopped

1 red onion, chopped

1–2 jalapeños, chopped

2 garlic cloves, minced

2 limes, juiced

1 teaspoon ground cumin

½ teaspoon chili powder

1 teaspoon salt

1 teaspoon ground pepper

2 (10-ounce) cans diced tomatoes and green chiles, such as Ro-Tel

1 (15-ounce) can diced tomatoes

In a blender, combine the tomatoes, cilantro, both onions, jalapeño, garlic, lime juice, cumin, chili powder, salt, and pepper. Blend on low until blended, but not pureed. Add both kinds of canned tomatoes. Pulse the blender until you have reached your desired consistency.

KID FAVORITE

MAKES
about 32 ounces
(1 quart)

TIME
20 minutes

SIDES AND DIPS

christmas eve spinach dip

This has made an appearance at every Christmas Eve in our family for as long as I can remember. It just isn't Christmas Eve without it. You can use crackers or tortilla chips to dip with this, but I prefer big soft chunks of sourdough bread!

1 (10-ounce) box frozen chopped spinach, thawed

1 (16-ounce) tub sour cream

1 cup mayonnaise

1 (8-ounce) can water chestnuts, drained and chopped

1 (1.4-ounce) packet vegetable recipe mix, such as Knorr

Salt and pepper, to taste

Round sourdough loaf, cut into chunks, for serving

Layer two paper towels on the counter and add the thawed spinach. Gather up the sides and squeeze over sink until all the water is wrung out.

In a large bowl, add the spinach, sour cream, mayonnaise, water chestnuts, and the vegetable recipe mix packet. Mix thoroughly. Taste and add salt and pepper as needed.

Cover the bowl with plastic wrap and refrigerate for at least an hour or up to 2 days. Serve with sourdough chunks.

SIDES AND DIPS

pumpkin spice dip

Not all dips have to be savory! This one is creamy, sweet, and perfectly spiced. Of course it can be a dip, but feel free to get creative with it as a cake filling or to sandwich gingersnap cookies together!

MAKES
approximately 3 cups

TIME
20 minutes

1 (8-ounce) package cream cheese, softened

1 (8-ounce) tub whipped topping, such as Cool Whip, defrosted

1 cup canned pumpkin puree

1 cup powdered sugar

2 tablespoons pumpkin pie spice blend, plus more for garnish

Apple slices, vanilla wafer cookies, and cinnamon pita chips, for serving

In the bowl of a stand mixer fitted with the whisk attachment, add the cream cheese, Cool Whip, pumpkin puree, powdered sugar, and pumpkin pie spice blend. Mix on medium speed until smooth and well combined.

Transfer to a medium bowl and sprinkle additional pumpkin pie spice blend on top. Serve with apples, vanilla wafers, and cinnamon pita chips.

INDEX

ABOUT THE AUTHOR

ELISE THOMAS is an entrepreneur, author, speaker, and the creative force and founder behind one of the fastest growing gourmet cookie franchises, Cookie Co. The company began in her home, but in August 2020, her first storefront opened in her hometown.

Three years later, Cookie Co. continues to expand their business throughout the US while upholding the same values of high quality, delicious flavor, and sourcing only the best ingredients.

Elise continues to be actively involved in the day-to-day operations of the business working alongside her husband, Matt. They are the proud parents of four amazing children who keep them on their toes. Whether she's multitasking in the office or keeping the family's busy schedule in check, Elise strives to balance her responsibilities with grace and integrity.